HOW TO BE A WINE EXPERT

Second Edition

by James M. Gabler

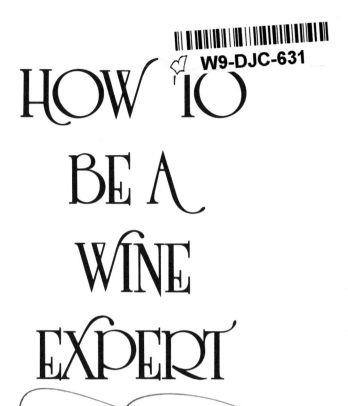

BACCHUS PRESS LTD.

Baltimore

Second Edition: 1995
Library of Congress Catalog Card Number 95-94317
International Standard Book Number 0-9613525-2-3

Cover design and maps by Wilma M. Rosenberger
Typesetting by Steven R. Meyer (the LetterEdge)

For information on ordering copies of this
book or other Bacchus Press publications call:
(410) 828-WINE (9463)

Published and Distributed by:
Bacchus Press Ltd.
1751 Circle Road
Baltimore, MD 21204
(410) 828-WINE (9463)
Fax: (410) 321-0763

TABLE OF CONTENTS

INTRODUCTION

For those with little time but a growing interest in wine, *How To Be A Wine Expert* provides a quick but thorough understanding of this fascinating subject. This book is not intended as an end-all to wine learning, for learning about wine is a never ending experience. Hopefully this book will pave the way for your exploring other wine trails that will lead to exciting adventures in taste and pleasure.

There are many people who genuinely enjoy wine but drink only a certain wine or wines. They are afraid to venture further, perhaps because they are intimidated by an aura of mystery and elitism with which some writers treat wine. Some beginning wine drinkers are so intimidated that they have been heard to say that "most wines taste the same." Even though some wines may look the same, they do not taste the same, and they do not smell the same.

Wine drinkers want to know how to taste the differences in wines, or why one wine is considered great and another ordinary. Unfortunately the most available source of information, wine books, is of little help. They tell you much about wine except what it smells and tastes like. It is not uncommon to read that the bouquet is "distinctly Riesling" or "scented with the Cabernet grape" or "typical of a great Burgundy." To call it "distinctly Riesling" or "scented with the Cabernet grape" does not describe the wine. What the reader wants to know is what is the scent of the Cabernet grape? What are the smell and taste characteristics of a great Burgundy?

This book classifies over 80 of the world's great wine varietals by color, smell and taste. Descriptions of smell and taste are, of course, subjective. Nevertheless, wines made from different or the same grapes, grown in different soils and different climates, have distinctly different smells and tastes. If you can taste the difference in foods, you can learn to taste the difference in wines. No claim is made for complete success, but it is a start into an aspect of wine that has been little explored.

After the name of each wine you will find the phonetic pronunciation; region or district of origin; principal grape variety; what the wine tastes and smells like; best clues for identifying the wine; when it should be drinking at its best; great, good and poor vintages; which foods best complement the wine; and the ideal temperature at which the wine should be served. The "Notes" cover salient facts about each wine along with the names of reliable wineries and producers. Here you will find not only the most famous producers but also wineries and producers who make good but inexpensive wines. In other words, good value for your money. The "Questions and Answers" cover a broad range of information.

Keeping wine notes is essential if you intend to develop your palate to the degree that you are able to translate smell and taste perceptions into an accurate judgment of what you are drinking and its relative value. It is recommended that when you find a really "wonderful" wine that you make a note of its name or soak off the wine label. If you don't, that "wonderful" wine will quickly fade from memory and you won't be able to enjoy it again.

Aside from the fact that over 55 additional wine varietals have been added to the Second Edition and all of the information updated, re-vised and expanded, there is another important change. The First Edition was published in 1987 and over that eight year period I have learned through the painful experience of having to pour down the drain too many old, dried-out wines that the aging potential for most quality red wines is shorter than generally recommended. Therefore, my "When To Drink" recommendations follow my experience as to when a particular wine varietal will be drinking at its best. If you keep wine too long, the fruit fades and it develops a "burnt" or "cooked" smell and taste and the remaining bottles are wasted, or, at best, barely drinkable. It is far better to drink a wine when it is a little too young and tannic but still full of fruit. Life really is too short to drink bad wine, so I suggest that you drink your wines sooner rather than later to determine when they are best suited to your taste. My guide on when to drink a wine is when it tastes good to me. When it reaches that point of personal satisfaction, why wait longer? How do you determine when a wine has reached this point of personal satisfaction? I suggest that you drink a bottle from time to time at home, at a wine tasting, at a restau-rant, at a friend's house, wherever. And remember, dry red and white wines almost always taste better when drunk with food.

Happy wine drinking!
Jim Gabler

WINE APPRECIATION

The appreciation of wine is an acquired taste. Although enjoyment and appreciation are related, they are not synonymous. It takes no special skill to drink a wine and know that you like it, even if you are not always able to tell why. As long as you like it, you can get enjoyment from wine without knowing anything about it. The same is true of art, music, ballet or most sensory experiences, but greater understanding will increase your satisfaction and appreciation. The same is true of wine. The more you know about it, the better you can understand it. To understand wine, you should read about it, talk about it, think about it and—drink it!

One of the best ways of acquiring a better understanding of wine is to taste it "blind," without knowing what is in the glass. Tasting wine blind forces the discipline and concentration of our senses that we otherwise take for granted. Not knowing what is in the glass causes us to become more sensitive to what it might be.

In judging wines, there are three evaluation keys that allow us to distinguish one wine from another: color, smell, often referred to as bouquet or aroma, and taste.

COLOR: The color of a wine is your first clue to its identity. To determine the color of a wine it helps to hold it to a light against a white background. In general, with white wines the deeper the color, the sweeter or older the wine. For example, a deep golden-hued wine in all probability is not a white Burgundy or Chablis. Conversely, a white wine with a pale yellow color with a tinge of green will never be a Sauternes.

Unlike white wines, red wines become lighter and browner in color as they acquire age. With red wines you should carefully examine the edge or rim of the wine in the glass. If it has a bluish tinge, it is probably a relatively young wine. A purple hue in a red wine also indicates youth and that it was probably made in a hot climate. This is a classic characteristic of many Californian, Australian, Italian and even French Rhône wines such as Côte Rôtie, Hermitage and Châteauneuf-du-Pape. but be careful, it can also be a Bordeaux or even a Burgundy produced in a very hot year. Browning at the rim indicates the wine in reaching or has reached maturity. If the wine is brown throughout it has probably passed it peak, although it still might be quite drinkable.

SMELL: Wine authorities claim correctly that the smell or bouquet of the wine is all they need to know—taste simple confirms the smell. In identifying wines, the smell is the most important clue. If you are to be successful in identifying wines, the smell or bouquet must be memorized. There is no short-cut. First it will seem confusing. You will wonder "Was the smell of cabbage a Bordeaux or a Burgundy?"; but, as you taste more, the confusion will clear up and the smell of cabbage, for example, will immediately register Burgundy. But remember this: if you instinctively or immediately think you have identified a wine by its bouquet, don't change your opinion.

TASTE: If you can't identify a wine from its color and bouquet, then you must rely on your taste. Here again, you must rely on your memory. Try to "tag" the taste of every wine you drink. Needless to say, recording your impressions will help. Here are some hints. Young Bordeaux are extremely tannic, so much so that they pucker the mouth. Burgundies, are lighter in body than Bordeaux, Côte Rôties, Hermitages, Châteauneuf-du-Papes and well made California Cabernet Sauvignons. Italian wines, particularly Barolos and Chiantis, have a distinctly harsh or bitter aftertaste. Chablis has an acidic tang and Sauternes a rich honeyed taste.

Being able to translate smell and taste perceptions into an accurate judgment of what you are drinking adds a significant dimension to both understanding and appreciation. Careful attention to the suggested colors, smells and tastes in the guide which follows will help you through this unfamiliar territory.

HOW TO READ THE GUIDE

WINE:
The name of the wine is followed by the phonetic pronunciation in parentheses.

REGION OR DISTRICT:
The wine region and district where the wine is produced.

PRINCIPAL GRAPE:
Because most wines are made from a blend of various grapes, the name of the principal grape from which the wine is made is given followed by the phonetic pronunciation in parentheses. Some wines are made from 100% of a particular grape. When this is the case, the name of the grape will be followed by "100%."

COLOR:
An attempt has been made to describe the most representative or "classic" color of each wine. However, descriptions ranging from "light to dark red" are necessary primarily because weather conditions vary from vintage to vintage. Using Château Lafite-Rothschild as an example, a comparison of the 1982 and 1980 vintages will point up the difference. Using the same mix of grapes from the same vines and employing the same vinification methods, Lafite made two different wines. With a perfect mixture of sun and rainfall, 1982 was a great vintage and 1982 Lafite is dark red and just now starting to drink at its "best" although a few more years of bottle age will improve it even further. 1980 was a poor year with cold, rainy weather. As a consequence, 1980 Lafite has a lighter color, was never a great wine and should have been drunk years ago.

BOUQUET:
A wine's bouquet is its most distinguishing feature. The descriptions given are based on the assumption that the wine has reached maturity. A wine that is drunk too young will not have developed its full bouquet characteristics. If drunk too old, its fruit will have faded and once the fruit is gone, it never returns.

TASTE:
Young red wines are often heavy with tannin which imparts an astringent and harsh taste to the wine. Tannin smooths out with proper bottle age. Aftertaste refers to the taste that is left in the

mouth after the wine has been swallowed and is a significant means of evaluating a wine. Great wines have pleasant, distinct and long-lasting aftertastes.

BEST CLUES:
This portion highlights one or two distinct characteristics of the wine to help you identify and remember the wine.

WHEN TO DRINK:
Wines made in great years take longer to develop than those made in good or poor years. There are three parts to this portion of the guide: Great, Good and Poor Years and which vintages fall in those categories. For example, in the red wines section under Burgundy, "Great Years" is followed by "3–12 years." The time span (3–12 years) represents how long the wine will keep, i.e., it can normally be drunk with satisfaction after 3 years but will keep for 12 years. Obviously, some Burgundies will be drinkable before the 3 year period and some will still be at the peak of perfection beyond 12 years, but it is a *safe* range. As a rule of thumb, good red wines, such as Volnay, Beaune, etc., should be drunk at the lower end of the scale (3–5 years), and the great reds, such as Chambertin, La Tache, etc., at the upper end (8–12 years). In good

years the time span is less. Very good vintages have been included in the great year category. It is my suggestion that you not buy wines of poor vintages unless you have a specific reason. Obviously, there are wines produced in poor vintages that stand out and represent good value. Nevertheless, there are too many good and great wines available that usually represent better value.

SERVE WITH:
Food with which the wines should be served should be varied to suit your taste. Nevertheless, experience has shown that certain wines are best complemented by certain types of food, and you are safe in following the suggestions.

SERVE AT:
The temperature at which the wines should be served are given in Fahrenheit degrees. Because of conservation efforts and increased fuel prices, many Americans have lowered their household temperatures to the 60°– 68°F range so room temperature now is an acceptable temperature to serve most red wines and avoids subjecting the wine to a cooling period in the refrigerator and the danger of over-chilling. Too cold a temperature masks the bouquet and flavor of wine, both reds and whites. In the case of white wine, a hour in a 39° refrigerator will

chill the wine to about 54° to 56°.

NOTES:
This portion points up salient features about the wines and includes the names of reliable wineries, shippers, producers and châteaux. The same wine, of the same year, selling for about the same price can vary enormously in quality depending upon the shipper or producer.

QUESTIONS AND ANSWERS:
These cover a wide range of information.

CALIFORNIA WINERIES:
California wineries are generally listed by the county in which a winery's principal place of business is located. There are exceptions, such as where wineries have developed reputations that are identified with a particular location such as those listed under Paso Robles rather than the county of San Luis Obispo.

INDEX:
Entries have usually been indexed in alphabetical order or as the name appears on the label. This is a break with the tradition of alphabetizing by last name. Examples: E. & J. Gallo and not Gallo, E. & J.; Angelo Gaja and not Gaja, Angelo, etc. Where "Chateau" and "Domaine" is a part of the vineyard or winery name, that vineyard or winery has been indexed under "Chateau" or "Domaine."

LIST OF MAPS

White Wine

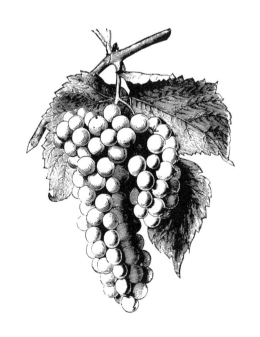

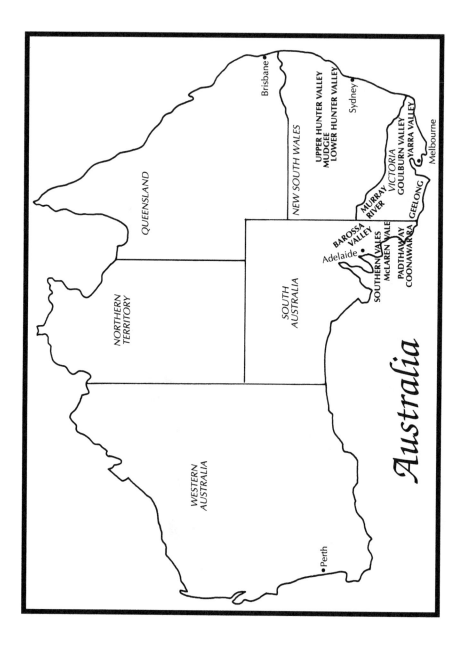

CHARDONNAY
(*Shar*-doe-nay)

REGION OR DISTRICT:
New South Wales; Victoria; South Australia.

PRINCIPAL GRAPE:
Chardonnay (*Shar*-doe-nay) 100%.

COLOR:
Pale to straw yellow.

BOUQUET:
Citrus; oaky; buttery; toasty.

TASTE:
Rich; medium-bodied; dry with good acidity and citric hints of lemon or grapefruit.

BEST CLUES:
Citrus nose with a hint of lemon on the taste and aftertaste.

SERVE WITH:
White meats, fish, shellfish, fowl.

WHEN TO DRINK:
Great and good years: 1–3 years (94, 93, 92).

SERVE AT:
50°–55°F.

NOTES: Australia has a tradition of wine making that goes back 175 years and that tradition is reflected today in the high quality of Australian wines. All of the great European *Vitis vinifera* grape varietals are grown here. The main white wines represented are Chardonnay, Gewurztraminer, Muscat, Riesling, Sauvignon Blanc and Semillon; the reds by Cabernet Sauvignon, Pinot Noir, Shiraz and Merlot.

Chardonnay has become the most popular white wine made in Australia and, like its California counterpart, it is not made for aging. It should be drunk young while still crisp and fruity.

Popular Chardonnay producers in **New South Wales** are Arrowfield, Brokenwood, Draytons, Lindemans, McWilliam's, Mitchelton, Rosemount Estate, Rothbury Estate, Saxonvale, Tyrrell's and Wyndham Estate.

Victoria: Brown Brothers, Coldstream Hills, Lindemans, Mildara, Mitchelton, Seppelt, Chateau Tahbilk.

South Australia: Black Opal, Chateau Reynella, Orlando Jacob's Creek, Leasingham, Lindemans, Mitchell, Oxford Landing, Penfolds,

Petaluma, Peter Lehmann, Rosemount Estate, Seppelt, Hardys, Wynns Coonawarra Estate, and Yalumba.

Q. What are the principal Australian wine regions?
A. There are three main wine regions that stretch out across the southeastern basin of Australia, and are separated by as much as 1000 miles: New South Wales, Victoria and South Australia. A fourth emerging wine region surrounds Perth in Western Australia.

Q. What other popular white wine is often blended with Chardonnay?
A. Semillon. In fact, you are more likely to find Semillon in combination with Chardonnay than by itself.

Q. Does Australia's downunder neighbor, New Zealand, make wines?
A. Yes. A full range of *Vitis vinifera* grapes are grown, and wines are made on both the North and South Islands. Because the growing climate is relatively cool, the white wines excel—especially Chardonnay and Sauvignon Blanc and exhibit high but balanced acid levels. Only a trickle are now found in the United States such as Cloudy Bay, Cooks, Cooper's Creek, Kumeu River, Montana and Morton Estate, but with their popularity growing more are arriving.

SEMILLON
(Sem-ee-*yon*)

REGION OR DISTRICT:
New South Wales; Victoria; South Australia.

COLOR:
Light to medium yellow.

TASTE:
Hint of lemon; touch of spice.

WHEN TO DRINK:
Great years: 1–5 years with claims for improvement for 10–20 years (94, 90, 88, 87, 86).
Good Years: 1–3 years (93, 92, 89).

PRINCIPAL GRAPE:
Semillon (Sem-ee-*yon*).

BOUQUET:
Slightly grassy when young; suggestion of lemon; with bottle age develops nutty, buttery, toasty scents.

BEST CLUES:
Slightly grassy with the hint of lemon on the palate; toasty scents.

SERVE WITH:
Seafood, chicken, light pastas, veal dishes.

SERVE AT:
50°–55°F.

NOTES: The Semillon grape, known in France for making the sweet wines of Sauternes, is usually made in Australia as a dry white wine. The best Semillons are made in three styles: dry with oak, dry without oak and sweet. It is claimed that dry Semillons need at least five years bottle age to reach maturity and sweet Semillons improve with even more age.

Some producers of this increasingly popular wine are:

New South Wales: Brokenwood, Lindemans, McWilliam's, Rosemount Estate, Rothbury Estate, Saxonvale, Seppelt, Tyrrell's, Wyndham Estate.

Victoria: Mitchelton, Tahbilk, Tisdall.

South Australia: Hardys, Henschke, Peter Lehmann, Mitchell, Penfolds, Yalumba.

BURGUNDY

REGION OR DISTRICT:
Burgundy.

COLOR:
Straw yellow, often with a hint of green.

TASTE:
Vanilla; hints of oak; spicy-fruit; dry with good body and balanced acidity; rich with a long aftertaste.

WHEN TO DRINK:
Great years: 2–6 years (92, 90, 89).
Good years: 2–3 years (94, 91, 88).
Poor years: (93).

PRINCIPAL GRAPE:
Chardonnay (*Shar*-doe-nay) 100%.

BOUQUET:
Buttery, toasty with crisp acidity; scent of oatmeal or hazelnuts or apples or lemon.

BEST CLUES:
Hints of oak; nut or fruit scented bouquet; rich and lingering after-taste.

SERVE WITH:
Fish, shellfish such as baked scallops, oysters, quenelles, veal, poultry.

SERVE AT:
50°–55°F.

NOTES: Along a three-mile stretch in the southern Côte de Beaune from Meursault (*Mere*-so) to Chassagne-Montrachet (Shass-*an*-ya Mawn-rasch-*shay*) come many of the world's greatest dry white wines. Within a radius of less than a mile are the five crown jewels. The undisputed king is Montrachet, surrounded by Chevalier-Montrachet (Chev-*al*-yea Mawn-rasch-*shay*), Bâtard-Montrachet (*Bah*-tar Mawn-rasch-*shay*), Bienvenues-Bâtard-Montrachet (Bee-*an*-vay new *Bah*-tar Mawn-rasch-*shay*) and Criots-Bâtard-Montrachet (*Cree*-o *Bah*-tar Mawn-rasch-*shay*).

Their main competition for the mantle of "the greatest dry white wine" is Corton-Charlemagne to the north. Many *Premiers Crus* of the highest quality also come from the vineyards surrounding the towns of Puligny-Montrachet (*Poo*-lean-ye Mawn-rasch-*shay*) and Chassagne-

Montrachet. Wines of equal quality are made just a short distance away to the north around the hamlet of Meursault.

Some highly reputable producers of fine white Burgundies are: Domaine Marquis-d'Angerville, Robert Ampeau, Joseph Drouhin, Domaine F. Gaunoux, Louis Jadot, Louis Latour, Domaine des Contes Lafon, Domaine Marc Morey, Domaine Leflaive, Bouchard, Remoissenet (Baron Thénard), Romanée-Conti, Domaine Ramonet.

Further to the south is Pouilly-Fuissé (*Poo*-ye *Fwee*-say). If you like Pouilly-Fuissé but find it a bit expensive, try the less expensive Saint-Veran (San Vay-*rawn*), or a Macon-Lugny (*Mac*-cawn *Loon*-ye), or a Macon-Village (*Mac*-cawn Vee-*lage*) made in the same general area as Pouilly Fuissé and from the Chardonnay grape.

Q. What is the Côte d'Or?
A. Côte d'Or (slope of gold) is a series of hills, some 36 miles in length that runs from just below Dijon in the north to Chalon-sur-Saône in the south.

Q. What is the Côte de Beaune?
A. It is the southern half of the Côte d'Or beginning north of the town of Beaune at Aloxe-Corton and ending at the village of Santenay in the south. Famous for its white Burgundies, it is also the vineyard region of such great red wines as Pommard, Volnay, Beaune and Le Corton.

Q. Where do the great white Burgundies come from?
A. All the Grand Cru white Burgundies come from the Côte de Beaune and account for about only 20% of that area's total production.

Q. What is the most expensive and arguably the best dry white wine in the world?
A. Le Montrachet, a Thomas Jefferson favorite.

Q. What is chaptalization?
A. Sugar is added to the must to increase the wine's alcohol content.

CHABLIS
(*Shab*-lee)

REGION OR DISTRICT:
France, Northern Burgundy.

COLOR:
Pale yellow with greenish tinge.

TASTE:
Bone dry to dry; mildly oaky;
acidic bite; light to medium body
with a crisp aftertaste.

WHEN TO DRINK:
Great years: 2–5 years (90, 89).
Good years: 2–3 years (93, 92, 91).
Poor years: (94).

PRINCIPAL GRAPE:
Chardonnay (*Shar*-doe-nay)
100%.

BOUQUET:
Flinty or slaty; apple-like.

BEST CLUES:
Flinty bouquet; bone dry taste
with crisp acidity.

SERVE WITH:
Oysters and all seafood.

SERVE AT:
50°–55°F.

NOTES: Nearly every wine producing country in the world has some
white wine called Chablis. Genuine Chablis, however, comes only from
a small delimited area in France surrounding the town of Chablis, southeast of Paris. There are four categories of Chablis: Grand Cru, Premier
Cru, Chablis and Petit Chablis which is rarely exported. Chablis Grand
Cru is the highest appellation and there are only seven vineyard areas
entitled to this designation—Blanchots, Bougros, Les Clos, Grenouilles,
Les Preuses, Valmur and Vaudésir. Premiers Crus wines are usually of
high quality and come from 40 vineyards that ring this tiny town. If
you wish to drink the best Chablis, your purchases should be confined
to the Grands Crus and Premiers Crus.

Some highly reliable shippers and producers are Domaine Auffray,
Jean-Claude Bessin, Jean Collet, René and Vincent Dauvissat, Jean
Defaix, J.P. Louis Droin, Marcel Duplessis, Jean Durup, Chateau Gre-
nouilles, Labouri-Roi, Laforet, Domaine Laroche, Roland Lavantureux,
Domaine Long-Depaquit, J. Moreau, Albert Pic, Francois and Jean-
Marie Raveneau, A. Regnard, Jacques Tremblay.

Q. Is Chablis considered a Burgundy wine?
A. Yes, although Chablis is physically separated from the Côte d'Or and Burgundy proper by 75 miles.

Q. Are wines that call themselves "Chablis" but made in some place other than around the town of Chablis, France, in any way related to real Chablis?
A. No. In fact most such wines in no way resemble or have anything in common with real Chablis, and calling them "Chablis" is simply an attempt to gain from the world reputation for quality that Chablis has established. The same applies to jug wines that are generically labeled "Burgundy, Chablis, Claret, Rhine," etc.

CHAMPAGNE
(Sham-*pain*)

REGION OR DISTRICT:
Ninety miles northeast of Paris.

COLOR:
Pale to yellow with persistent small bubbles. A limited amount of Rosé is made.

TASTE:
Crisp and tangy; frothy bubbles persist and prickle the mouth; tart and slightly acidic.

WHEN TO DRINK:
Vintage Champagne within 3–10 years of the vintage date; non-vintage when bottled although some connoisseurs are of the opinion that non-vintage Champagne gains complexity and style with 2 or 3 additional years of bottle age.
Vintage years: *Great years* (90, 88, 85, 82); *Good years* (89, 86, 83).

PRINCIPAL GRAPE:
Pinot Noir (*Pee-no Nawhr*) and Chardonnay (*Shar*-doe-nay) and Pinot Meunier (*Pee-*no *Moo-*nee-ay).

BOUQUET:
Suggestive of a fine white burgundy; toasty; oaky; spicy; yeasty.

BEST CLUES:
The persistence of small bubbles in the glass and in the mouth; a distinct toasty, yeasty bouquet and taste.

SERVE WITH:
Brut (dry) Champagne as an aperitif, fish, shellfish, creamy cheeses; sweet Champagne with desserts or as an aperitif.

SERVE AT:
50°F.

NOTES: Charles Dickens called Champagne one of the elegant extras of life and the world seems to agree. True Champagne is made from a blend of red and white grapes grown in France's most northern vineyards around Rheims and Épernay. Two fermentations are required to achieve its spritely bubbles. First it is fermented out dry, like any table wine. After the wine has been bottled, sugar and yeasts are added causing it to again ferment in the bottle. The sugar is converted into almost equal parts of alcohol and carbon dioxide gas which is absorbed into the wine and creates the bubbles.

This second fermentation creates a sediment, so the bottles are placed neck down in slanting racks and periodically shaken and turned causing the sediment to eventually form in the neck of the bottles. Before Champagne is shipped, the degorgement or sediment removal takes place. The wine in the neck of the bottle is frozen and the sediment removed. To replace the degorged wine, a dosage or mixture of wine and sugar is added. The amount of sugar added to the dosage determines whether the Champagne is to be brut (extra dry), extra sec (dry), sec (slightly sweet), demi-sec (sweet) or doux (very sweet).

Although vintage Champagne is made in outstanding years, most Champagne is a blend of wine from various years. Each Champagne house has its own style that ranges from full-bodied to light-bodied. Bollinger, Krug, Pol Roger and Veuve Clicquot-Ponsardin are houses that produce full-bodied Champagnes. Deutz, Laurent-Perrier, Moët & Chandon, Mumm, Perrier-Jouët, and Louis Roederer produce medium-bodied wines. The style of making delicate and light-bodied Champagne is followed by Piper-Heidsieck, Pommery, Taittinger, and Nicolas Feuillatte.

California: High quality sparkling wines are made in California by more than 50 wineries including S. Anderson, Domaine Carneros, Domaine Chandon, Chateau St. Jean, Codorniu Napa, Culbertson, Maison Deutz, Gloria Ferrer, Handley, Kornell, Iron Horse, Jordan, Korbel, Mirassou, Robert Mondavi, Domaine Mumm Napa Valley, Piper Sonoma, Roederer Estate, Scharffenberger, Schramsberg, and Wente Bros.

Spain's Cavas (wineries) produce millions of bottles of quality sparkling wines with Codorniu and Freixenet being the two largest Cavas most frequently seen on the American market.

Q. Has Champagne always been a sparkling wine?
A. No. It was a still wine until the 17th century when a Benedictine Monk named Dom Perignon is credited with developing the Champagne method of putting bubbles in the bottle.

Q. Champagne is made from what grapes?
A. Only three grapes are allowed, the white Chardonnay and two black grapes, Pinot Noir and Pinot Meunier. Champagne is usually a blend of these grapes.

Q. The words "Blanc de Blanc" on a Champagne label mean what?
A. That the Champagne in the bottle is made from 100% white Chardonnay grapes.

Q. Should still wines be shaken and turned while they are aging?
A. No! Still wines should age without interference. The only wines that are shaken and turned while in the bottle are Champagne and sparkling wines made in the Champagne method.

Q. Should you store an opened bottle of Champagne for a day or two?
A. Not unless you have to. Champagne does not keep beyond a reasonable drinking time after being opened. The bubbles disappear and it loses its sparkle and goes flat, so drink it up.

Q. How should you keep Champagne and for how long?
A. Champagne is sold after an aging process and, except for vintage Champagne, is ready to drink when released. This doesn't mean, however, that you have to drink it up immediately. Champagne will keep for 3 or 4 years but, in my opinion, extensive bottle age causes it to lose its sparkle and taste. Like all wines (except those with screw caps) it should be stored on its side so that the cork stays in contact with the Champagne. Vintage Champagne should be drunk within 3 to 10 years of its vintage.

Q. Do most Champagnes carry a vintage date?
A. No. Most Champagne is non-vintage, a blend of wines from several years. A small percentage of Champagne in special years is vintaged, meaning a blend of wines made from the best grapes of a superior year. Vintage Champagne costs more.

Q. How should you open Champagne and other sparkling wines?
A. A flying cork can be dangerous so never point the bottle toward anyone when opening. Always slant the bottle at a 45° angle and away from other people. Before opening, place a towel or cloth over the cork and the bottle neck. Untwist and remove the wire hood. With the towel still over the cork, grasp the cork with one hand and twist the bottle in the other hand in a slow and easy motion. The towel will keep the cork from flying across the room.

CONDRIEU
(*Cawn*-dree-uh)

CHATEAU GRILLET
(*Shat*-toe Gree-*yea*)

REGION OR DISTRICT:
Northern Rhone, just south of
Vienne.

COLOR:
Pale gold with tinges of green.

TASTE:
A dry wine with a hint of apricots
and peaches and a touch of spice;
hint of almonds.

WHEN TO DRINK:
Great years: 1–3 years (94, 91,
90).
Good years: 1–3 years (93, 92).

PRINCIPAL GRAPE:
Viognier (Vee-*ahn*-yea).

BOUQUET:
Apricots; fresh flowers that echo
the Riesling grape.

BEST CLUES:
Floral bouquet.

SERVE WITH:
Freshwater fish, white meats,
mild cheeses.

SERVE AT:
50°–55°F.

NOTES: The wines of Condrieu and Chateau Grillet (7.5 acres) are located just down-stream from the vineyards of Côte Rôtie. They are not found in the average wine store because of their limited production and popularity in France. Still, they do trickle onto the shelves of certain wine merchants so keep an eye out for them. They are expensive, especially Chateau Grillet, but are quality wines that have a floral bouquet and a taste different from any other dry white wine you are acquainted with, and that alone is reason enough to want to try them. These are wines to be drunk within three years of their vintage.

Quality Condrieu producers found in the United States include Chapoutier, Domaine du Chêne, Yves Cuilleron, J. M. Gerin, E. Guigal, Domaine Pichon, André Perret, Patricia Porte, J. Y. Multier's Chateau du Rozay, Herve Richard, René Rostaing, Georges Vernay, Vidal-Fleury.

Q. Is the Viognier grape grown anywhere else than in France?
A. Yes, in California a growing number of wineries make wines from the Viognier grape. Here are some to look for: Alban Vineyards, Arrowood, Beringer, Calera, Callaway, Eberle, Field Stone, Kunde, Jade Mountain, La Jota, Preston, Richie Creek, Edmunds St. John, Bonny Doon *Le Sophiste*, McDowell, Joseph Phelps *Vin du Mistral*, R. H. Phillips, Qupé, Rabbit Ridge, and Sierra Vista.

GEWÜRZTRAMINER
(Guh-*vertz*-trah-*mee*-ner)

REGION OR DISTRICT:
Alsace in northeast France and separated from Germany by the Rhine River.

COLOR:
Medium yellow.

TASTE:
Dry; flowery-spicy; moderate acidity and alcohol; pungent aftertaste.

WHEN TO DRINK:
Great years: 2–5 years (90, 89).
Good years: 1–3 years (94, 93, 92, 91).

PRINCIPAL GRAPE:
Gewurztraminer 100%.

BOUQUET:
Very spicy; nutmeg; mace; cinnamon; pungent; clove-like.

BEST CLUES:
Spicy or clove-like bouquet.

SERVE WITH:
Fish and seafood with rich sauces, chicken, oriental cusine, smoked salmon and other smoked meats.

SERVE AT:
50°–55°F.

NOTES: Except for a little red wine made mainly from the Pinot Noir grape, all Alsatian wines are white. They are sold under the name of the grape from which they are made. The best Alsatian wines are usually labeled Cuveé Prestige, Cuveé Reserve, Reserve Personnelle or Grand Cru followed by the name of the grape, i.e, Gewurztraminer, Riesling, Sylvaner, etc.

The first-time drinker of Gewurztraminer is often put off by the overpowering spiciness of the bouquet and taste. Although not a wine for everyone, it has an individuality of bouquet and taste that makes it unique.

The following is a list of producers who make consistently fine Gewurztraminers: Lucien Albrecht, J. Becker, Léon Beyer, Bott Frères, Jos. Meyer, Clos St. Landelin, Dopff and Irion, Dopff "Au Moulin," Hugel, Marc Kreydenweiss, Kuentz-Bas, Gustave Lorentz, Domaine Ostertag, Landmann-Ostholt, Schlumberger, Domaine Schoffit, Sick-Dreyer, Pierre Sparr, Trimbach, Domaine Weinbach, and Zind Humbrecht, but you should not be afraid to purchase lesser known labels for the general quality of Alsatian wines is quite high.

Q. Are all Alsatian wines white?
A. No. A little red and rosé is made from the Pinot Noir and Pinot Meunier.

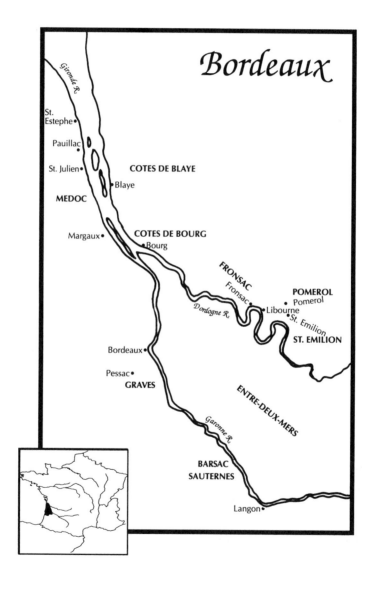

GRAVES
(Grahv)

REGION OR DISTRICT:
South of Bordeaux.

COLOR:
Straw yellow to gold.

TASTE:
Faintly metallic or steely; dry to semi-sweet; lacks acidity or bite; light crisp body; tart aftertaste.

WHEN TO DRINK:
Great years: 2–4 years (94).
Good years: 1–3 years (93, 91, 90).
Poor years: (92).

PRINCIPAL GRAPE:
Sauvignon Blanc (So-veen-*yawn* Blawn) and Semillon (Say-mee-*yawn*).

BOUQUET:
Earthy-spicy; figs; apricots; herbs; a whiff of fresh-cut grass.

BEST CLUES:
Slight scent of fresh-cut grass; herbs.

SERVE WITH:
Alone as an aperitif, or with seafood and white meats.

SERVE AT:
50°–55°F.

NOTES: Although this region is best known for its great red wines, especially Châteaux Haut-Brion and La Mission-Haut-Brion, a little more than a third of its production is white wines. Although there is a consistency of character with white Graves, there is a variance in styles depending mainly on the blends of the two principal grapes, Semillon and Sauvignan Blanc. The quality of white Graves has improved over the past ten or so years. Some of the best are: Châteaux Bouscaut, Carbonnieux, de Fieuzal, Haut-Brion Blanc, La Louvière, Laville-Haut-Brion, Malartic-Lagravière, Olivier, Smith-Haut-Lafitte, and Domaine de Chevalier.

Q. What is A.O.C. or, more formally, Appellation d'Origine Contrôlée?
A. It is a group of French laws that strictly define the appellations of

origin in an attempt to protect the quality of French wines, to protect the consumer from false labeling, and to protect the wine grower from unscrupulous competitors.

Q. Should you look for Appellation Contrôlée on the label when choosing a French wine?
A. Yes. It doesn't guarantee that you are going to like the wine, but it attempts to insure its origin and that the wine has met certain standards.

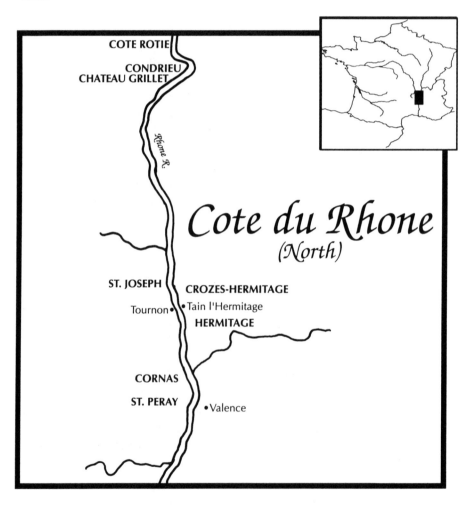

HERMITAGE
(Air-mee-*taj*)

REGION OR DISTRICT:
Northern Rhône.

COLOR:
Lemon yellow; yellow-gold.

TASTE:
Dry and alcoholic; rich flavor
with apricot edge; lemony; low
acidity; full-bodied.

WHEN TO DRINK:
Great years: 2–5 years (91, 90,
89).
Good years: 1–3 years (94, 93, 92).

PRINCIPAL GRAPE:
Marsanne (Mar-*sahn*) and
Roussanne (Roo-*sahn*).

BOUQUET:
Apricot scent with alcoholic
overtones; nutty.

BEST CLUES:
Apricot scent and lack of acidity.

SERVE WITH:
Seafood, freshwater fish, veal,
pork, ham, turkey.

SERVE AT:
55°–58°F.

NOTES: White Hermitage is not well known in this country and that's our loss because it's a quality wine. Although lacking the crisp acidity of a Chablis, it is a full-bodied, dry wine that can be drunk young, but gains in quality with some age. There are few wines, if any, that go as well with ham.

Fine examples are M. Chapoutier's Chante-Alouette, Paul Jaboulet Ainé's Chevalier de Stérimberg, Jean-Louis Chave, J. L. Grippat, E. Guigal, H. Sorrel.

Q. Is the Rhone Valley the only wine region where the Marsanne is grown?
A. No. The Marsanne grape is grown in the Southern Rhone, Langue-doc, Provence, Switzerland, and by some vintners in California. But nearly 70% of wines made from the Marsanne grape come from two Australian wineries, Chateaux Tahbilk and Mitchelton, both located in the Goulburn Valley, Victoria.

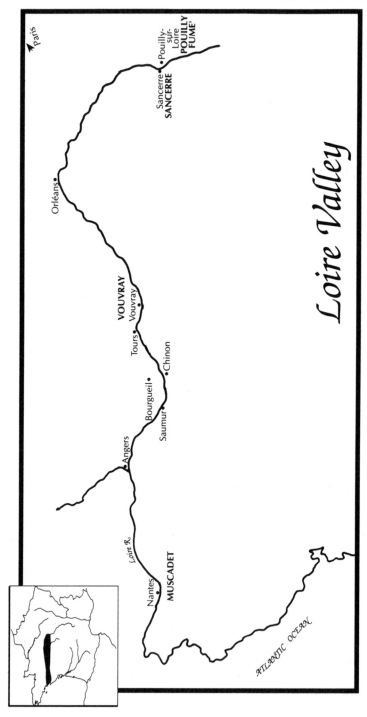

MUSCADET
(Muss-ka-*day*)

REGION OR DISTRICT:
Lower Loire (Lwahr) around the city of Nantes in western-central France.

COLOR:
Pale straw-yellow.

TASTE:
Dry, light, with crisp acidity, usually without oak, with a tart or slightly bitter finish.

WHEN TO DRINK:
Muscadets do not improve with age and should be drunk within one or two years of the vintage. 1994 was a good vintage.

PRINCIPAL GRAPE:
Muscadet (Muss-ka-*day*).

BOUQUET:
A scent of minerals, musky, touch of vanilla.

BEST CLUES:
Crisp and dry with a musky bouquet.

SERVE WITH:
Oysters and shellfish, poached fish.

SERVE AT:
48°–52°F.

NOTES: The city of Nantes is near the Atlantic Ocean and the vineyards extend almost to the ocean. The main vineyard region is Sevre-et-Maine and these are the Muscadets most commonly found in the United States, and the wines to look for. This region lies between the Sevre and Maine Rivers before they join the Loire at Nantes. You will sometimes see *sur lie* on the label meaning after fermentation the wine was left in the vat *sur lie* (on the lees) and bottled shortly afterward, allowing the newly fermented wine to gain an extra measure of fruit and body. Muscadet wines go well with seafood, and for those who like a light dry wine, they often represent the best value for your money on a wine list. Muscadet should be drunk young.

Some better known producers are: André-Michel Brégeon, Chateau La Noë, Chateau de la Ragotiere, Chateau du Cléray, Chateau du Coing de St. Fiacre, Domaine de la Batardiere, Domaine de la Pepiere, Domaine de la Quilla, Louis Métaireau, Marquis de Goulaine, Robert Michele, Henri Poiron, and Marcel Sautejeau.

PINOT BLANC
(*Pee*-no Blawn)

REGION OR DISTRICT:
Alsace, Northeastern France.

PRINCIPAL GRAPE:
Pinot Blanc (*Pee*-no Blawn).

COLOR:
Pale yellow.

BOUQUET:
Suggestion of honey; apples; rich tropical fruit.

TASTE:
Dry, apple-like, no oak.

BEST CLUES:
Rich tropical fruit; lack of oak.

WHEN TO DRINK:
Great and good years: 1–2 years (94, 93, 92, 91).

SERVE WITH:
White meats and seafoods.

SERVE AT:
45°–50°F.

NOTES: Although Alsatian wines come in flute shaped German bottles, their taste is distinctly dry. Unlike other French wine regions, here the wine is identified by the name of the grape used to make it. When it comes to value for money and versatility there are few wines that can equal the Pinot Blanc from Alsace.

Well known producers of Pinot Blanc are J. B. Adam, Lucien Albrecht, J. Becker, Léon Beyer, Marcel Deiss, Dopff & Irion, Dopff "Au Moulin," René Dopff, Hugel, Marc Kreydenweiss, Landmann-Ostholt, Gustave Lorentz, Jos. Meyer, Mittnacht-Klack, Domaine Ostertag, Charles Schlerer, Schlumberger, Sick-Dreyer, Pierre Sparr, Trimbach, Domaine Weinbach, A. Willm, and Zind Humbrecht.

Q. Are all Alsatian wines dry?
A. Most are but not all. Vendange Tardive (late harvest) wines are sweet, and wines labeled Selection de Grains Noble are sufficiently sweet that they fit into the dessert category. Do not choose a Vendange Tardive or Selection de Grains Noble for your meal unless you want a sweet wine.

PINOT GRIS
(*Pee*-no Gree)

A/K/A TOKAY D'ALSACE

REGION OR DISTRICT:
Alsace, Northeastern France.

COLOR:
Yellow.

TASTE:
Dry, pear-like; rich, full-bodied, creamy texture with a hint of honey on the aftertaste.

WHEN TO DRINK:
Great years: 1–4 years (94, 93, 90, 89).
Good years: 1–2 years (92, 91).

PRINCIPAL GRAPE:
Pinot Gris (*Pee*-no Gree) 100%; also called Tokay D'Alsace.

BOUQUET:
Smokey or musky; buttery with apricot overtones; a whiff of almonds.

BEST CLUES:
Smokey, apricots, creamy.

SERVE WITH:
Grilled salmon, seafood, white meats, pork, veal.

SERVE AT:
50°–55°F.

NOTES: In Alsace the Pinot Gris is more popularly called Tokay D'Alsace which should not be confused with the sweet wine from Hungary known as Tokay because they are totally dissimilar in taste, origin and grape varietal. Although Alsatian Pinot Gris is a dry wine, there often is a touch of sweetness on the taste and aftertaste.

Outstanding producers are Jean Baptiste Adam, J. Becker, Léon Beyer, Dopff & Irion, Marc Kreydenweiss, Kuehn, Schlumberger, Pierre Sparr, Trimbach, Domaine Weinbach, Zind Humbrecht.

Q. What other white wines are made in Alsace?
A. Sylvaner, Muscat and Crémant (Sparkling). You probably won't run

into the Sylvaner on an American restaurant wine list because it is the lesser wine of this region, but in Alsace most restaurants carry it. It is an inexpensive, light, refreshing, easy to drink wine that goes well with the local food. The Muscat in Alsace is dry and full-bodied with a fresh, grapey taste and can be enjoyed as an aperitif. Crémant or sparkling wines are popular in Alsace and should be better known here because they are excellent.

Q. How do Alsatian winemakers designate their special wines?
A. They are labeled Cuvée Prestige, Cuvée Réserve or Réserve Personnelle. In the 1980s, 47 vineyards were designated "Grand Cru," so if the wine comes from any of these vineyards, that too will be noted on the label.

Q. What is a major difference between Alsatian Pinots and French, California, and Australia Chardonnays?
A. The absence of oak. In Alsace the winemaker usually does not oak-age his wines.

Q. In what other countries or wine regions does the Pinot grape excel?
A. In other parts of France as the Pinot Beurot, and Malvoise; in Germany as the Rülander; in Italy as the Pinot Grigio; and in Oregon as Pinot Gris.

Q. What basic information should a wine label give you?
A. The name of the wine, the country and region of production, the vintage, the name of the producer, the alcohol content by volume.

Q. What is the largest wine producing country in the world?
A. Italy, followed by France and Spain.

RIESLING
(*Rees*-ling)

REGION OR DISTRICT:
Alsace, Northeastern France.

COLOR:
Pale straw.

TASTE:
Dry; wet stones; slight suggestion of pineapple or citrus.

WHEN TO DRINK:
Great years: 1–5 years (93, 90).
Good years: 1–2 years (94, 92, 91).

PRINCIPAL GRAPE:
Riesling (*Rees*-ling) 100%.

BOUQUET:
Suggestion of lemon, scent of flowers, minerals.

BEST CLUES:
Floral bouquet.

SERVE WITH:
Fish, oysters, mussels, pork, veal, white sausages and white meats.

SERVE AT:
48°–52°F.

NOTES: Alsatian Riesling is a different breed than the sweet-tasting wines of its German neighbors. In Alsace these wines are dry and crisp with elegant scents and concentrations of flavors that make it the natural accompaniment to the foods of this region. In great vintages it has the style, breed and elegance that should allow it to take its place with most of the world's great dry white wines and, yet, it remains largely ignored and unknown to the wine-drinking public. If you like dry white wines with your meals, give an Alsatian Riesling a try. It will give you a different taste experience, and that's a part of learning about wine.

Here are some Alsatian producers who make quality Rieslings: J. B. Adam, Lucien Albrecht, Léon Beyer, Albert Boxler, Bott Frères, Rolly Gassmann, Marcel Deiss, Dopff and Irion, Dopff "Au Moulin," Domaine Ostertag, Hugel, Marc Kreydenweiss, Gustave Lorentz, J. Luc Mader, Jos. Meyer, Schlumberger, Pierre Sparr, Trimbach, Domaine Weinbach, and Zind Humbrecht.

SANCERRE
(Sawn-*sair*)

POUILLY-FUMÉ
(*Poo*-ye *Foo*-may)

REGION OR DISTRICT:
Upper Loire Valley.

COLOR:
Pale gold to golden, often with a touch of green.

TASTE:
Dry, light to medium body. Crisp, refreshing with balanced acidity; hint of liquorice; hint of vanilla on the aftertaste with acidic bite.

WHEN TO DRINK:
Great and good years: 1–3 years (94, 93, 92, 90).
Poor years: (91).

PRINCIPAL GRAPE:
Sauvignon Blanc (So-veen-*yawn* Blawn).

BOUQUET:
Asparagus; gun-flint; steely; herbal; lemon; cut grass.

BEST CLUES:
Asparagus; herbs.

SERVE WITH:
As an aperitif or with shellfish, fish, white meats, mild cheeses.

SERVE AT:
48°–50°F.

NOTES: The villages of Sancerre and Pouilly are on the upper Loire River. Both wines are made from the Sauvignon Blanc grape and grown on chalk hills. Sancerre and Pouilly Fumé are similar in bouquet and taste.

Some of the better known producers of Sancerre are: Domaine Henri Bourgeois, Paul Cotat, Lucien Crochet, Pierre et Alain Dezat, Pascal Jolivet, Alphonse Mellot, André Neveu, Comte Lafond de Ladoucette, Michel Redde, Jean Reverdy, and André Vatany.

Fine producers of Pouilly Fumé are: Domaine A. Cailbo, Jean-Pierre Chamoux, Didier Dagueneau, Chateau Favray, Domaine Denis Gaudry, Mandry, Masson-Blondelet, Michel Redde, and Chateau du Nozet-Ladoucette.

SAUTERNES
(Saw-*tairn*)

REGION OR DISTRICT:
Sauternes.

COLOR:
Golden; browning with age.

TASTE:
Honeyed; caramel, sweet but not cloying with balanced acidity and good body; rich but sometimes a slightly bitter finish.

WHEN TO DRINK:
Great years: 5–20 years (90, 89, 88, 86, 83, 76, 75).
Good years: 3–10 years (94, 91, 85, 82, 81, 80, 79, 78).
Poor years: (94, 93, 92, 87, 84).

PRINCIPAL GRAPE:
Sémillon (Say-mee-*yawn*) and Sauvignon Blanc (So-veen-*yawn* Blawn).

BOUQUET:
Honey-like; figs; pears; apricots; vanilla.

BEST CLUES:
Honey-like bouquet.

SERVE WITH:
Foie gras at the beginning of a meal or strawberries or other fruit desserts at the end; also after dinner by itself or with a Roquefort or other type bleu-cheese.

SERVE AT:
50°–55°F.

NOTES: The wines of Sauternes are considered by many wine connoisseurs to be the greatest sweet white wines on earth. The glory of this region is Château d'Yquem (*Shat*-toe-dee-kem). Three-quarters of a century before the French classification of 1855, Thomas Jefferson had chosen Château d'Yquem the best Sauternes. Château d'Yquem, which had pleased many of Jefferson's dinner guests, changed its taste somewhat sixty years after his visit because of *Botrytis cinerea* (the noble rot), the mildew that covers the grape. The story of its discovery is that in 1847, the Marquis de Lur-Saluces, the owner of Château d'Yquem (and still owned by the same family), returned from Russia late and found that the grapes had been attacked by a rot. Nevertheless he ordered that they be picked and pressed. The wine obtained was of such high quality that its fame quickly spread and the noble rot became desirable. Today the crop is picked bunch by bunch as it reaches the desired degree of ripeness. At Château d'Yquem this process can require 8 or more separate pickings.

Other outstanding Sauternes, including its neighboring parishes of Barsac, Preignac, Bommes and Fargues, are Châteaux Coutet, Climens, Rieussec, Suduiraut, La Tour Blanche, Lafaurie-Peyraguey, Guiraud, Sigalas-Rabaud, Nairac, Doisy-Daene, Raymond-Lafon, and Filhot.

Q. What are the principal grape varietals that make Sauternes?
A. Sémillon, Sauvignon Blanc and sometimes, a little Muscadelle. Château d'Yquem plants about 80% Sémillon and 20% Sauvignon Blanc.

Q. How long has the Sémillon been a Sauternes grape varietal?
A. The Sémillon has been the principal grape of the Suaternes area since the 1st century.

Q. What is *Botrytis cinerea* and what causes it?
A. *Botrytis cinerea*, sometimes called the noble rot, is a mold that attaches to the grapes and shrivels and dehydrates them so that their sugar becomes concentrated. Botrytis is caused by a combination of humidity, fog and temperatures that allow the mold to develop.

Q. What do the words *mis en bouteille au Chateau* mean?
A. It means the wine has been bottled on the property where the grapes were grown. It is referred to as "chateau bottled."

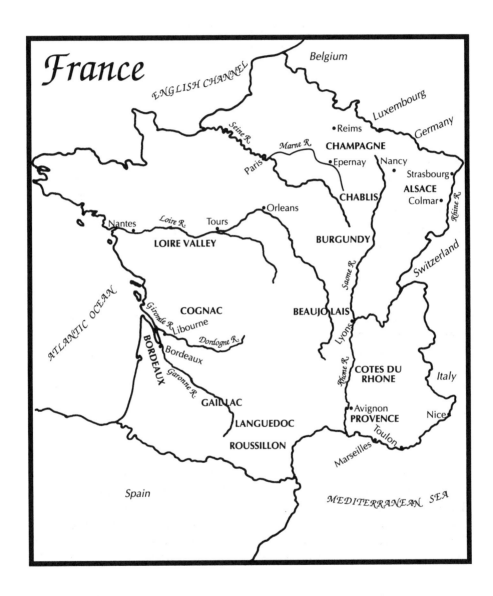

VOUVRAY
(Voov-*ray*)

MONTLOUIS
(Mawn-lew-*ee*)

REGION OR DISTRICT:
Loire Valley near Tours.

COLOR:
Pale to medium yellow.

TASTE:
Varies from dry to semi-sweet and sweet with moderate to high acidity. Also a rich sparkling Vouvray is made.

WHEN TO DRINK:
Great and good years: (94, 93, 92, 90). Dry Vouvrays within 1–5 years; sweet Vouvrays within 3–10 years.

PRINCIPAL GRAPE:
Chenin Blanc (Shay-*nan* Blawn).

BOUQUET:
Honey; scents of hay; sweet Vouvray has hints of tropical fruits.

BEST CLUES:
High acidity.

SERVE WITH:
Sweet Vouvrays as an aperitif or with desserts. Dry Vouvrays (less frequently found in America) go well with seafood, fish, goat cheeses.

SERVE AT:
50°–55°F.

NOTES: The towns of Vouvray and Montlouis lie just east of the city of Tours and the grapes are grown on chalky hills overlooking the Loire River—Vouvrary on one side and Montlouis on the other. Vouvrary and Montlouis range in styles from table wines through sparkling wines, from bone dry through many shades of sweetness. Therefore, before ordering or buying a Vouvrary or Montlouis, find out first whether the wine is dry or sweet.

Some well-known producers or shippers of Vouvrays are Marc Brédif, Chateau Moncontour, Domaine Bourillon "Vielles Vignes," Domaine Debrenial, Dudier Champalow, Pierre Foreau, Gaston Huet, J.M. Monmousseau, Deaplessie-Mornay, Pichot, and Prince Poniatowski.

LIEBFRAUMILCH
(Leeb-frau-*milsh*)

REGION OR DISTRICT:
It is made in four German wine regions: Nahe, Rheingau, Rheinhessen, and Pfalz.

COLOR:
Usually light, pale straw.

TASTE:
Mild and sweet.

WHEN TO DRINK:
Drink it young. It does not improve with bottle age.

PRINCIPAL GRAPE:
Varied.

BOUQUET:
Floral.

BEST CLUES:
Sweet taste with a floral aroma.

SERVE WITH:
Seafood, white meats, or by itself.

SERVE AT:
45°–50°F.

NOTES: Liebfraumilch is well known to most of us and, though sales have fallen over the years, it still has a large following in the United States. Liebfraumilch is not made from any specific grape. It is a generic wine, so when you order it, be prepared for a mild, sweet or semi-sweet wine. Since so much depends on the producer's style, your best guide to quality is the name of the shipper or producer.

Here are some well-known Liebfraumilch labels: Black Tower, Blue Nun, Hanns Christof, Glockenspiel, Kaiser, and Madonna.

Q. What is Süssreserve and what is it used for?
A. It is a sweet pasteurized grape juice that many producers add back to their fully fermented wines to achieve what they consider the proper degree of sweetness. The use of Süssreserve has been legal in Germany since 1959 and is widely used.

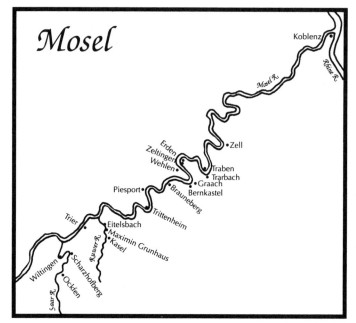

MOSEL
(Mo-*zell*)

REGION OR DISTRICT:
Mosel-Saar-Ruwer.

PRINCIPAL GRAPE:
Riesling (*Rees*-ling) 100%.

COLOR:
Pale yellow with greenish tinge.

BOUQUET:
Scented and flowery; apple; melon.

TASTE:
Fruity and perfumed; crisp acidity with balanced sweetness. Fresh and slightly apple-like; light body; crisp finish.

BEST CLUES:
Floral bouquet; fruity with crisp acidity.

SERVE WITH:
Fish, oysters and other shellfish, mild sausages, or alone.

WHEN TO DRINK:
Great years: 3–5 years (94, 93, 90, 89, 88).
Good years: 2–4 years (92, 91).
Poor years: (87).

SERVE AT:
52°–58°F.

NOTES: German wines are classified in 3 categories: Tafelwein (table wine and rarely exported), Qualitätswein (quality wine) and Qualitätswein mit Prädikat (QMP) (quality wine with distinction). There are six grades of Qualitätswein mit Prädikat (Kual-ee-*tates*-vine mit Pred-*ee*-kat): Kabinett (Kab-*ee*-net) slightly sweet; Spatlese (*Shpait*-lay-zuh) sweet; Auslese (*Ows*-lay-zuh) honey sweet; Beerenauslese (*Bearen*-ows-lay-zuh) very sweet; Trockenbeerenauslese (Trock-en-bearen-ows-lay-zuh), intensely sweet, and Eiswein (very sweet). Regardless of the degree of sweetness, a fine Mosel wine is always kept in balance by crisp acidity. Kabinett, because it is the driest, goes best with a meal.

The Mosel River along with its two small tributaries, the Saar and the Ruwer, comprise an important German wine area. German wine connoisseurs claim that each rivers' vineyards produce wines with subtle differences, yet retain strong family resemblances. Mosels are greenish in color, light in body, with a fruity acidity and floral bouquet. They are best enjoyed young.

Mosels of world fame include: Maximim Grunhauser Abtsberg and Herrenberg; Trittenheimer Apotheke; Eitelsbacher Karthauserhofberg; Scharzhofberger; Piesporter Goldtropfchen; Bernkasteler Doctor and Badstude; Wehlener Sonnenuhr; Brauneberger Juffer; Ockfener Bockstein; Graacher Himmelreich; Ürziger Wurzgarten; Erdener Prälat and Treppchen; Zeltingen Sonnenuhr. There are many other fine producers of Mosel-Saar-Ruwer wines so don't be afraid to venture away from this list.

Q. Are all Mosel wines made from the Riesling grape?
A. All the great Mosels are, but there has been a trend in the Mosel away from the Riesling and toward the easier to grow Muller-Thurgau grape.

Q. In addition to the Rheingau and Mosel-Saar-Ruwer, what are the other major German wine producing regions?
A. There are eleven other major wine regions: Mittelrhein, Ahr, Nahe, Rheinhessen, Pfalz, Franken, Hessische-Bergstrasse, Wurttemberg and Baden, plus two new regions, Saale-Unstrut and Sachsen.

Q. What are some of the differences in style and taste between Mosel and Rheingau Riesling wines?
A. Rheingaus are richer and fuller-bodied. Mosels are more delicately structured with crisp acidity.

Q. Are all German wines white?
A. No. A small amount of red wine is made from the Spatburgunder (Pinot Noir) grape but because of the colder German climates, it does not achieve the bouquet or develop the body and depth of flavor of French Burgundies or California or Oregon Pinot Noirs.

Q. Does Germany make sparkling wines?
A. Yes. It is known as Sekt and the best Sekt is made from the Riesling grape. There is no delimited Sekt region in Germany such as Champagne in France and it is made throughout the German wine country.

RHEINGAU
(*Rhine*-gow)

REGION OR DISTRICT:
Rheingau.

COLOR:
Light to gold yellow.

TASTE:
Sweet with balanced acidity;
flowery and fruity; more body
and less acidity than a Mosel.

WHEN TO DRINK:
Great years: 3–10 years (94, 93,
92, 90, 89, 88).
Good years: 2–5 years (91).
Poor years: (87, 86).

PRINCIPAL GRAPE:
Riesling (*Rees*-ling) 100%.

BOUQUET:
Flowery, perfumed and forth-
coming.

BEST CLUES:
Big perfumed bouquet.

SERVE WITH:
Chicken, veal, seafood, fish or
alone.

SERVE AT:
55°F.

NOTES: The Rheingau is generally conceded by all except Mosel fans to be Germany's finest wine region. The most famous estates and vine-yard areas of the Rheingau are Schloss Johannisberg, Schloss Rein-hartshausen, Schloss Vollards, Steinberger, Schloss Schonborn, Schloss Eltz, Marcobrunn, Hochheim and Rudesheim.

Rheingaus of great years labeled Qualitätswein mit Prädikat im-prove with bottle age and the Beerenausleses and Trockenbeerenaus-leses need great age—10 to 25 years—to reach their zeniths. Unfortu-nately they are extremely expensive.

Q. What does "Hock" mean and where did it originate?
A. Hock has become a generic term used by the English to signify German wines. Its name derives from the village of Hochheim, located 10 miles east of the Rheingau proper and overlooking the Main River. Hochheim's most famous vineyard is Domdechaney.

Q. What food goes best with Auslese, Beerenauslese, or Trockenbeer-enauslese?
A. These sweet wines are best served as aperitifs but can also be matched with fruits, fruit desserts, and paté.

Q. What is the Rheingau?
A. A vineyard region on the right bank of the Rhine that stretches from Rudesheim to Hochheim.

Q. What is the largest German wine producing region?
A. Rheinhessen. Its most famous wines come from vineyards that face the Rhine and are known by the names of the towns they surround: Oppenheim, Nierstein, Nackenheim, Bodenheim and Laubenheim.

Q. Do German wines improve with bottle age?
A. The sweeter varieties do but most should be drunk when they are young and fresh. Kabinetts and Spätleses by top producers in outstanding vintages often improve with 2 to 4 years of bottle age, especially Rheingaus. Ausleses, Beerenausleses and Trockenbeerenausleses of great vintages are even more age-worthy, but I caution that you drink even these wines progressively (a bottle from time to time).

Q. Do all German wines come in flute shaped bottles?
A. All except for the wines of Franken, which come in squat, green flagon-like bottles called bocksbeutel (box-boy-tl). Franken wines are not often seen in the United States and that's our loss because they are the dryest of the German wines with an almost Chablis quality to them.

Q. What is Eiswein (Ice-vine)?
A. It is a sweet wine made from grapes that were picked while frozen on the vines.

Q. What are some other legendary vintage years in Germany that would be relevant to age-worthy Beerenausleses and Trockenbeerenausleses?
A. 1971, 1976, and 1983 were great vintages.

Q. What is the most famous Rhinegau vineyard?
A. Schloss Johannisberg.

Q. What do the great Mosel vineyards look like?
A. They are some of the steepest in the world. Hundreds of years of human labor have transformed sheer slate cliffs into hanging vineyards by means of terraces. There is a saying in the Mosel that "where machines can go, no grapes should grow."

Q. What foods go best with German wines?
A. If your palate likes a bit of sweetness in your meal-time wines, German wines will serve you well. Germans seem to enjoy their wines best as aperitifs or after the meal.

Q. How can you tell from looking at a German wine label whether the wine in the bottle has been made from the Riesling grape?
A. The wine producer will almost always place on the label, "Riesling."

Q. What is residual sugar?
A. During fermentation the grape sugar is changed to almost equal parts of alcohol and carbon-dioxide. The portion that is not converted and remains in the wine is called residual sugar or residual sweetness.

PINOT GRIGIO

•Milan   **SOAVE**
Verona•

Turin
•
**ASTI
SPUMANTE**

•
Bologna

•Florence

VERDICCHIO

ORVIETO

EST! EST!! EST!!!

•Rome
FRASCATI

•Naples

*Italian
White Wines*

ASTI SPUMANTE
(Ass-tea Spu-*mahn*-tea)

REGION OR DISTRICT:
Piedmont, northwest Italy.

COLOR:
Water pale to pale straw.

TASTE:
Foaming bubbles with varying
degrees of sweetness.

WHEN TO DRINK:
As soon as released. Freshness
and youth are the essence of Asti
Spumante's appeal.

PRINCIPAL GRAPE:
Moscato d'Asti (Mos-*cot*-toe
Das-*tea*) or Moscato di Canelli.

BOUQUET:
Aromatic; grapey.

BEST CLUES:
Sweet, fresh and grapey.

SERVE WITH:
By itself or with desserts.

SERVE AT:
45°–50°F.

NOTES: Asti Spumante takes its name from the town of Asti in the Piedmont region of northwest Italy. Spumante is the Italian word for foaming or sparkling. Asti Spumante is a sweet, foaming, grapey wine that at its best is fresh and easy to drink. It has found a world following, particularly in Italy, United States, Germany, and England. It is usually made in bulk with only one fermentation (see Champagne for a different method of obtaining the bubbles) and is always sweet to some degree.

Some well-known producers are: Villa Banfi, Cinzano, Folonari, Fontanafredda, Fratelli Gancia, Granduca, Martini & Rossi, Michele Chiarlo, Riunite, Santini, Tosti, and Zonin.

Q. What change took place with Asti Spumante in 1994?
A. It was given DOCG status.

FRASCATI
(Frahs-*cot*-tea)

REGION OR DISTRICT:
Latium: Castelli Romani, west-central Italy just southeast of Rome.

COLOR:
Water pale to pale straw.

TASTE:
Light-bodied; dry; crisp and fruity; refreshing acidity; hint of apricots.

WHEN TO DRINK:
Within 1–3 years of the vintage.

PRINCIPAL GRAPE:
Malvasia (Mal-vas-*ee*-ah) and Trebbiano (Treb-be-*ahn*-o).

BOUQUET:
Faintly nutty; a slight suggestion of liquorice.

BEST CLUES:
Dry and crisp with a faintly nutty bouquet.

SERVE WITH:
Shellfish, fish, pastas with white sauces, white meats.

SERVE AT:
45°–55°F.

NOTES: For centuries Frascati was the favorite wine of the Popes. Today its existence is threatened by Rome's urban sprawl. Frascati is always white and comes in three styles: dry (seco), semi-sweet (amabile), and sweet (cannellino). Dry Frascati is the most popular and the type discussed above. But when ordering, be on the safe side and ask whether it is dry or sweet.

One of the best Frascatis found in the United States is Antonio Pulcini's Colli di Catone's Colle Gaio. Other well-known Frascati producers are Campobello, Fontana Candida, Pallavicini, San Matteo, Villa Romana, and Villafranca.

Q. What Frascati is the first choice of restaurants?
A. The overwhelming favorite is Fontana Candida whose best label is Santa Teresa.

GAVI
(*Gah*-vee)

CORTESE DI GAVI
(Cor-*tay*-zay dee *Gah*-vee)

REGION OR DISTRICT:
Piedmont, northern Italy.

COLOR:
Straw yellow with hints of green.

TASTE:
Dry, light-bodied; crisp with light citrus fruit and an acidic bite.

WHEN TO DRINK:
Within 1–3 years of the vintage.

PRINCIPAL GRAPE:
Cortese di Gavi (Cor-*tay*-zay dee *Gah*-vee).

BOUQUET:
Fresh and appley; sometimes lemony.

BEST CLUES:
Hints of citrus with an acidic bite.

SERVE WITH:
Fish, shellfish, and white meats.

SERVE AT:
45°–50°F.

NOTES: Gavi takes its name from a small town in southwest Piedmont located in the Monferrato hills. This dry white wine has become fashionable of late and is relatively expensive.

The most popular Gavi on restaurant wine lists is Villa Banfi's Principessa. Other popular versions are Bersano, La Bollina, Contratto, Fasciola Broglia, Figini, Fontanafredda, Giacosa Fratelli, Marchese Di Barolo, Martinengo, Soldati's La Scolca, and Volpi.

Q. What white wine from Latium is better known for its name than its quality?
A. EST! EST!! EST!!! from Montefiascone, north of Rome. Two fine producers of this light, easy to drink wine are Falesco and Mazziotti.

ORVIETO
(Or-vee-*ate*-toe)

REGION OR DISTRICT:
Umbria, central Italy, between
Florence and Rome.

COLOR:
Pale straw to light gold.

TASTE:
Both dry (seco) and sweet
(abbaccato or amabile).

WHEN TO DRINK:
Great and good years: within 1–3
years of the vintage. Orvietos
don't improve with age, so drink
them young.

PRINCIPAL GRAPE:
Trebbiano (Treb-be-*ahn*-o).

BOUQUET:
Varies depending on whether dry,
semi-sweet or sweet. Dry Orvietos
are the wines usually sold in the
United States. A hint of almond
on the nose.

BEST CLUES:
Hints of almonds in the bouquet
and taste.

SERVE WITH:
As an aperitif, fish, shellfish,
fish, pasta fagioli, pasta with
vegetables.

SERVE AT:
45°–50°F.

NOTES: Although Orvieto comes in two styles, dry (seco) and sweet
(abbaccato), dry Orvieto is what is usually found in the United States,
but to be on the safe side ask if the bottle you are buying is dry or sweet.

Some of the best known producers are Antinori's Castello della Sala,
Luigi Bigi, Boscaini, Campogrande, Cecchi, Melini, Poggio del Lupo,
Ruffino, Vaselli.

Q. Some Orvieto has on the label "Classico." What does that mean?
A. That the wine was made from grapes harvested inside the original
growing zone and generally superior in quality.

PINOT GRIGIO
(*Pee*-no Gree-gee-oh)

REGION OR DISTRICT:
Friuli and Alto Adige and other wine regions in Italy.

PRINCIPAL GRAPE:
Pinot Grigio (*Pee*-no Gree-gee-oh).

COLOR:
Water pale to pale straw.

BOUQUET:
Smokey, hints of spice.

TASTE:
Ripe fruit; hint of grapefruit or lemon; suggestion of sweetness in the aftertaste.

BEST CLUES:
Smokey bouquet and ripe fruit.

SERVE WITH:
Fish, shellfish, chicken, pasta in white sauces, white veal dishes and other white meats.

WHEN TO DRINK:
Pinot Grigio should be drunk young when it is fresh—within 1 to 3 years of its vintage. 1994 was an excellent vintage.

SERVE AT:
45°–50°F.

NOTES: Pinot Grigio is one of the best known white wines of Italy and a member of the famous Pinot family of grapes. Pinot Grigio is grown and produced in several Italian wine regions but it excels in Friuli, located in the northeast corner of Italy bordering Austria and what was formerly Yugoslavia. Although a full range of red, white and sparkling wines are made in Friuli, Pinot Grigio is the best known wine from this region. Another wine region that produces outstanding Pinot Grigio is Alto Adige located north of Verona.

The following is a list of well-known producers, some from wine regions other than Friuli and Alto Adige: Armani, Bargo Conventirmani, Bollini, Bortoluzzi, Castello Banfi, Girolamo Dorigo, Franco Furlan, La Cadalora, La Castellada, La Marca, Livio Felluga, Lungarotti, Maso Poli, Mezzacorona, Muzic, Pighin, San Angelo, Santa Margherita, Sartori, Terlano, Tiefenbrunner, Valdadige, Valfieri, Villanova, Villa Frattina, Zenato, and Zuc Di Volpe.

SOAVE
(*Swa*-vay)

REGION OR DISTRICT:
Veneto, just northeast of Verona
and bordering Valpolicella in
northern Italy.

COLOR:
Light gold.

TASTE:
Light and with a hint of almonds
and a slightly bitter finish.

WHEN TO DRINK:
Within 1–3 years of the vintage.

PRINCIPAL GRAPE:
Garganega (Gar-*gahn*-eh-ga) and
Trebbiano (Treb-be-*ahn*-o).

BOUQUET:
Fruity with the suggestion of
almonds.

BEST CLUES:
Hint of almonds on the nose.

SERVE WITH:
Light pastas, fish, chicken, veal.

SERVE AT:
45°–50°F.

NOTES: Soave's relatively low alcoholic content and clean, crisp taste makes it easy to drink. The best Soaves are made from grapes grown on the hills surrounding the village of Soave just northeast of Verona. This is known as the Classico zone. Soave Classico costs more but it is worth the difference in price because it is usually a better wine.

Here are some of the best known producers: Anselmi, Bertani, Bolla, Boscaini, Folonari, Masi, Milafiore, Pasqua, Pieropan, Santa Sofia, Sartori, Cantina Sociale di Soave.

Q. What Soaves are most frequently found on restaurant wine lists?
A. Anselmi and Bolla.

Q. What do the words "Cantina Sociale di Soave" mean when found on the bottle label?
A. That the wine was produced by a cooperative—one of the largest in Italy.

VERDICCHIO
(Vair-*dee*-key-o)

REGION OR DISTRICT:
Marches, central-northeast Italy
bordering the Adriatic Sea.

COLOR:
Pale straw with a hint of green.

TASTE:
Dry, light-bodied with a refreshing lemony acidity and rich, ripe
fruit; a suggestion of salt or
minerals with a slightly bitter
aftertaste.

WHEN TO DRINK:
Great and good years: Within 1–3
years of the vintage.

PRINCIPAL GRAPE:
Verdicchio (Vair-*dee*-key-o).

BOUQUET:
Lemon; minerals; hint of melon.

BEST CLUES:
Crisp lemon acidity with a
slightly bitter aftertaste.

SERVE WITH:
Fish, shellfish, white meats, even
slightly spicy foods.

SERVE AT:
50°–55°F.

NOTES: Verdicchio is one of the best white wines of Italy. It is made in
the region of Marches, about halfway down Italy's east coast and along
the Adriatic Sea. The best Verdicchios come from an area called Castelli di Jesi, a DOC zone. Bottles labeled "Classico" are from grapes
produced in vineyards historically considered the best. The wine is
shipped in a green vase-like bottle.

Some well-known producers are: Fratelli Bisci, Bucci, Colonnara,
Fazi-Battaglia, Garofoli, Umani Ronchi, and Zaccagnini.

Q. Which of the above Verdicchios is most frequently found on restaurant wine lists?
A. Fazi-Battaglia.

CHARDONNAY
(*Shar*-doe-nay)

REGION OR DISTRICT:
California.

COLOR:
Light to medium yellow.

TASTE:
Appley fruit; dry but rich with moderate acidity; vanilla can give sweet impression; slightly spicy aftertaste.

WHEN TO DRINK:
Great years: 1–3 years (94, 93, 91, 90).
Good years: 1–2 years (92, 89).

PRINCIPAL GRAPE:
Chardonnay (*Shar*-doe-nay), usually 100%.

BOUQUET:
Apple-like; toasty oak; rich tropical fruit; buttery; vanilla.

BEST CLUES:
Toasty oak; rich tropical fruit; moderate acidity.

SERVE WITH:
White meats such as fowl, fish, shellfish, fowl, oysters, and scallops.

SERVE AT:
52°–55°F.

NOTES: Some of the best dry white wines in the world are being made from the Chardonnay in California's Napa, Sonoma and Mendocino Counties and the Central coast areas of Monterey, Paso Robles and Santa Barbara. In blind tastings they have proved worthy competitors for even the best white Burgundies. Many are aged in Burgundian oak barrels.

High on the list of well-made Chardonnays are:
El Dorado: Lava Cap.
Lake County: Guenoc and Konocti.
Livermore Valley: Concannon and Wente Bros.
Marin: Kalin.
Mendocino: Fetzer, Handley, Jepson, and Parducci.
Monterey: Chalone, Cronin, Jekel, Chateau Julien, Morgan, Monterey Vineyards, Robert Talbott, and Ventana.

Napa: Acacia, S. Anderson, Beringer, Burgess, Cakebread, Chateau Montelena, Clos du Val, Clos Pegase, Consentino, Cuvaison, Costello, Far Niente, Flora Springs, Folie á Deux, Franciscan, Freemark Abbey, Girard, Goosecross, Grgich Hills, Hawk Crest, Heitz, Hess Collection, Robert Keenan, Markham, Louis M. Martini, Merryvale, Peter Michael, Joseph Phelps, Robert Mondavi, Monticello, Mt. Veeder, Newton, Napa Creek, Quail Ridge, Raymond, Rombauer, Rutherford Hill, St. Clement, St. Supéry, Saintsbury, V. Sattui, Schug, Sequoia Grove, Signorello, Silverado, Robert Simskey, Spring Mountain, Shafer, Stag's Leap Wine Cellars, Sterling, Stonegate, Stony Hill, Sutter Home, Swanson, Trefethen, Truchard, Villa Mt. Eden, Chateau Woltner, and ZD Winery.

Paso Robles: Baron, Creston, Eberle, Meridian, Tobin James and Wild Horse.

San Benito: Calera.

San Luis Obispo: (Arroyo Grande and Edna Valleys): Baileyana, Edna Valley, and Talley.

Santa Barbara: Au Bon Climat, Babcock, Byron, Cambria, Firestone, Foxen, Gainey, Fess Parker, Qupé, Sanford, Santa Barbara Winery, Vita Nova, and Zaca Mesa.

Santa Clara: J. Lohr and Mountain View.

Santa Cruz: Cinnabar, Thomas Fogarty, Mount Eden, and Ridge.

Sonoma: Alderbrook, Alexander Valley, Arrowood, B.R. Cohn, Belvedere, Benziger, Buena Vista, Chalk Hill, Chateau De Baun, Chateau St. Jean, Chateau Souverain, Clos du Bois, De Loach, Domaine Michel, Domaine St. George, Dry Creek, Glen Ellen, Gary Farrell, Geyser Peak, Ferrari-Carano, J. Fritz, Handley, Hanzell, Iron Horse, Jordan, Kendall-Jackson, Kenwood, Kistler, Lambert Bridge, Landmark, MacRostie, Marimar Torres Estates, Peter Michael, Matanzas Creek, Mazzocco, Mill Creek, Murphy-Goode, Pedroncelli, Rabbit Ridge, St. Francis, Chateau St. Jean, Sebastiani, Seghesio, Sonoma-Cutrer, Simi, Rodney Strong, Taft Street, M.G. Vallejo, and Viansa.

Temecula: Callaway.

Yolo: R. H. Phillips.

Yuba: Renaissance Vineyard and Winery.

Q. When the wine is named for a varietal such as Chardonnay or Cabernet Sauvignon, what does this mean to the consumer?
A. The wine must contain a minimum of 75% of that grape varietal. Up to 25% of other grapes may be added.

CHENIN BLANC
(*Shay*-nan Blonk)

REGION OR DISTRICT:
California.

PRINCIPAL GRAPE:
Chenin Blanc.

COLOR:
Straw to pale gold.

BOUQUET:
Melon; honeysuckle; figs;
suggestion of vanilla.

TASTE:
Crisp, mineral tastes that range
from dry to sweet with most
being semi-sweet.

BEST CLUES:
Melon bouquet with semi-sweet
to sweet taste.

WHEN TO DRINK:
When released or within 1 to 2
years of the vintage date. 1990
through 1994 were very good to
excellent vintages.

SERVE WITH:
As an aperitif or with fish,
scallops and white meats such
as chicken, turkey, and veal.

SERVE AT:
45°–52°F.

NOTES: Chenin Blanc (also see Vouvray) is a popular wine grape in California and used extensively for blending. The wines range from dry to sweet but most are made in the "off-dry" style and contain some residual sugar which means that they are sweet in some degree. Most Chenin Blancs spend little or no time in oak, although a few wineries do ferment the wines out dry and oak-age them. Chenin Blanc should be drunk young when its fruit flavors are at their best.

The following is a list of well-known Chenin Blanc producers:
Amador: Story Winery and Charles Spinetta.
El Dorado: Gold Hill and Windwalker.
Lake County: Guenoc.
Mendocino: Fetzer, Husch, and Parducci.
Monterey: Emerald Bay, Monterey Vineyards, and Ventana.
Napa: Beringer, Chappellet, De Moor, Folie à Deux, Girard, Inglenook, Charles Krug, Milat, Robert Mondavi Woodbridge, Pine Ridge,

Stag's Leap Wine Cellars, Sutter Home, and Villa Mt. Eden.
   Paso Robles: Martin Brothers.
   Santa Barbara: Foxen and Santa Barbara.
   Santa Cruz: Mirassou.
   Sonoma: Alexander Valley, Hacienda, Davis Bynum, Dry Creek, Kenwood, Preston, Simi and Windsor.
   Temecula: Callaway.
   Yolo: R.H. Phillips.

Q. With Chenin Blanc should you pay attention to vintages?
A. Yes. If the wine carries a vintage year then you should always try to select a wine made in a good or great year.

Q. Where is Temecula?
A. Temecula is a wine region located about 45 minutes by car northeast of San Diego.

Q. Can I drink sweet wines with my meals?
A. If you like sweet wine with your meals, there is no reason you should not have what you want. But there are so many wine and food experiences to be had that it would be self-limiting not to try other wines—dry, red, white, rosé, semi-sweet, sweet, sparkling, etc.

Q. Do smoked foods go best with dry wines or slightly sweet wines?
A. Obviously personal preference should be your guide, but wines with a touch of residual sugar seem to balance well with smoked foods as does the spiciness of a Gewurztraminer.

Q. What does the pH in wine mean?
A. pH describes exactly how acidic, or non-acidic, a wine is and represents the concentration of hydrogen ions in wine. The lower the pH the higher the acidity.
   Wine pH usually falls between 3.1 and 3.6 with white wines at the lower end and red wines at the higher end.

Q. In what order should wines be served?
A. As a general rule: Dry white before dry red; young before old; dry before sweet.

GEWÜRZTRAMINER
(Guh-*vertz*-trah-me-ner)

REGION OR DISTRICT:
California.

COLOR:
Medium yellow to gold.

TASTE:
Usually some degree of spicy sweetness.

WHEN TO DRINK:
Great years: 1–5 years (94, 93, 92, 91, 90).
Good years: 1–3 years (89).

PRINCIPAL GRAPE:
Gewurztraminer (Guh-*vertz*-trah-me-ner).

BOUQUET:
Spicy; floral; cloves; apricot.

BEST CLUES:
Spicy and somewhat sweet.

SERVE WITH:
Rich appetizers such as patés, smoked meats, spicy Oriental or Indian foods, baked ham.

SERVE AT:
45°–50°F.

NOTES: Gewurztraminer has been grown in California for more than 100 years and is still popular with winemakers throughout the state. In Alsace it is dry; in California it usually has a perceptible sweetness and is probably best enjoyed as an aperitif or dessert wine. Wherever it is grown, the Gewurztraminer has an over-powering spiciness of bouquet and taste and you either like it or you don't, and the best way to find out is to drink it. When drinking it for the first time, at home is the place to make your decision.

Some wineries make what they call a late harvest Gewurztraminer and the style of this wine is distinctly sweet—at least the equivalent of a German Auslese.

Some of the better known California producers of Gewurztraminer are:

Mendocino: Adler Fels, Fetzer, Handley, Husch, Lazy Creek, Navarro, Parducci.

Monterey: Chateau Julien, Chouinard, Ventana.

Napa: Beringer, Bouchaine, Mont St. John, Napa Ridge, Joseph Phelps, Round Hill and Sutter Home.

Santa Cruz: Bargetto and Thomas Fogarty.

Santa Barbara: Babcock and Firestone.

Sonoma: Alderbrook, Alexander Valley Vineyards, Adler Fels, Buena Vista, Chateau St. Jean, Clos du Bois, De Loach, Geyser Peak, Gundlach-Bundschu, Handley, Hop Kiln, St. Francis, Chateau St. Jean, Stonestreet, Windsor and Z. Moore.

Q. Is Gewurztraminer made in Oregon and Washington?

A. Yes. Not too many Oregon wineries make it a top varietal, but two that do are Foris and Weisinger. It is more popular in Washington where it is a significant varietal from the following wineries: Biscuit Ridge, Hinzerline, Charles Hooper, Mont Elsie, Seth Ryan, Tucker Cellars and Manfred Vierthaler.

Q. When the words "produced and bottled by" appear on the label in California, what does it mean?

A. That at least 75% of the wine was fermented by the winery named on the label.

Q. If a specific region or viticultural area such as Napa or Sonoma appears on the wine label, what does it mean?

A. That 85% of the grapes used to make that wine were grown in that region.

Q. What kind of wine should you reject if presented to you at a restaurant?

A. Any wine that has a bad odor or a sour or metallic flavor. Wine should smell and taste like wine, not smell of rotten socks or locker rooms or taste sour or burnt. You should reject any wine that is presented already opened. Insist on seeing the wine opened at your table. There are a number of things that can happen to cause a wine to go bad, but the most common cause is that the wine becomes oxydized as a result of too much air contact. Oxydized or "maderized" wines have a burnt or cooked smell and taste. Getting a "maderized" bottle of wine is one of the hazards you run when you accept a bottle that has been opened out of your presence.

JOHANNISBERG RIESLING
(Joe-hahn-nis-berg *Rees*-ling)

REGION OR DISTRICT:
California.

COLOR:
Pale straw to medium yellow.

TASTE:
Fruity with some degree of
sweetness.

WHEN TO DRINK:
Great years: 2–4 years (94, 92,
91, 90).
Good years: 1–3 years (93, 89).

PRINCIPAL GRAPE:
Riesling (*Rees*-ling) 100%.

BOUQUET:
Floral perfumes; peach; apricots;
pineapples.

BEST CLUES:
Floral bouquet with some degree
of sweetness on the palate.

SERVE WITH:
Rich flavored and spicy foods
such as Indian and Oriental
dishes, baked ham, turkey,
chicken, or by itself as an aperitif.

SERVE AT:
45°–50°F.

NOTES: Whether labeled White Riesling or Johannisberg Riesling, it is the same grape that produces the great Mosels and Rheingaus of Germany. In California, however, it can be sweet, dry, or anywhere in between.

A number of wineries produce overripe or botrytised wines with sugar levels equaling German Ausleses and Beerenausleses. These are sweet and should be enjoyed as aperitifs or with dessert. Other wineries produce what is labeled "Late Harvest Rieslings" from overripe grapes with high sugar and low acid levels. These intensely sweet wines can be identified by the terms "Late Harvest," "Selected Late Harvest," "Special Select Late Harvest" on their labels and, as a rule of thumb, the more words used the sweeter the wine.

Some California producers of quality White Riesling or Johannisberg Riesling wines are:

Lake County: Guenoc and Wildhurst.

Livermore Valley: Concannon, Retzlaff, and Wente Bros.

Mendocino: Fetzer, Greenwood Ridge and Hidden Cellars.

Monterey: Jekel and Ventana.

Napa: Beringer, Chateau Montelena, Franciscan, Freemark Abbey, Inglenook, Long, Robert Mondavi, Rutherford Vintners, Stag's Leap Wine Cellars, and Trefethen.

Santa Barbara: Fess Parker, Firestone, Gainey, Santa Ynez Winery and Zaca Mesa.

Santa Clara: J. Lohr.

Santa Cruz: Mirassou, Sycamore Creek.

Sonoma: Chateau St. Jean, Grand Cru, Gundlach Bundschu, Kendall-Jackson, Pedroncelli, Sebastiani and Windsor.

Temecula: Callaway.

Yuba: Renaissance.

Q. Are California dessert wines made from grapes other than Riesling?
A. Many California wineries are making delicious dessert wines from a variety of grapes. For example, Quady Winery in Madera makes two orange Muscats, Essensia and Electra and a red dessert wine called Elysium. Chateau De Baun in Sonoma makes a sweet wine called Symphony by crossing the Muscat Alexandria and Grenache Gris.

Q. Should desserts be sweeter than the wine served with them?
A. No. If the dessert is too sweet, it will overwhelm the wine's sweetness giving the wine a bland taste.

Q. Do white wines and cheese go together?
A. Generally they don't because the high fat content in most cheeses tends to overpower the bouquets and flavors of white wine. But if you like cheese with white wine, have it.

SAUVIGNON BLANC
(So-veen-*yawn* Blonk)

A/K/A FUMÉ BLANC
(*Foo*-may Blonk)

REGION OR DISTRICT:
California.

COLOR:
Light to medium yellow.

TASTE:
Spicy; herbaceous with a crisp tangy and dry aftertaste of lemon.

WHEN TO DRINK:
Great years: 1–3 years (94, 93, 92, 91, 90).
Good years: 1–2 years.

PRINCIPAL GRAPE:
Sauvignon Blanc, usually 100%.

BOUQUET:
Fresh cut grass; lemon; herbal scents; asparagus; thyme; melon; fig.

BEST CLUES:
Grassy bouquet like the smell of a freshly cut lawn.

SERVE WITH:
Shellfish, fish, white meats, poultry, ham, goat cheese, spicy foods.

SERVE AT:
55°F.

NOTES: The quality of California Sauvignon Blanc (also called Fumé Blanc by some wineries) has improved immensely in the past five or so years. Although it is produced in different styles, well made Sauvignon Blancs have a consistent identifying hallmark—a grassy bouquet that some equate to the smell of "fresh mowed grass." Sauvignon Blanc is also the principal grape varietal that makes the dry white wines of Graves and the rich flavored Sancerre and Pouilly Fumé wines from the Upper Loire Valley. It goes well with a wide range of foods.

The following wineries make quality Sauvignon Blancs:
Amador: Karly.
El Dorado: Lava Cap.
Lake County: Guenoc and Konocti.

Livermore: Concannon.

Marin: Kalin.

Mendocino: Handley, Hidden Cellars, Husch, Jepson and Parducci.

Modesto: E & J Gallo.

Monterey: Chateau Julien, Morgan, Monterey Vineyards, and Ventana.

Napa: Beaulieu, Beringer, Cakebread, Caymus, Duckhorn, Frogs Leap, Flora Springs, Markham, Merryvale, Robert Mondavi, Newton, Robert Pecota, Robert Pepi, Joseph Phelps, Round Hill, St. Clement, St. Supéry, V. Sattui, Signorello, Silverado, Spottswoode, Stag's Leap Wine Cellars, Sterling, Stonegate, St. Clement, and Sutter Home.

Santa Barbara: Byron, Santa Barbara Winery, Firestone and Gainey.

Sonoma: Adler Fels, Alderbrook, Benziger, Buena Vista, Carmenet, Chalk Hill, Chateau St. Jean, Clos du Bois, Dry Creek, Ferrari-Carano, J. Fritz, Geyser Peak, Lambert Bridge, Handley, Hanna, Iron Horse, Kendall-Jackson, Kenwood, De Loach, Matanzas Creek, Murphy-Goode, Pedroncelli, Preston, Quivira, Rochioli, Sebastiani, Seghesio, Simi, Rodney Strong and Windsor.

Temecula: Callaway.

Yolo: R. H. Phillips.

Yuba: Renaissance.

Q. What can I expect when I visit Napa Valley?

A. Napa Valley is a north-south corridor about 30 miles long and less than 4 miles wide at its widest. It is surrounded by mountains to the east, west and north. Two highways travel its length, State Highway 29 through the heart of the Valley and the more scenic and less congested Silverado Trail along its eastern border. Vineyards and wineries are everywhere and most of them welcome visitors. There are many places to stay overnight ranging from luxury resorts to bread and breakfast lodging and a variety of first-class restaurants.

Q. Where should wine be stored?

A. Ideally it should be stored in a room, closet, cabinet or cellar that is cool, dark and free of vibrations, and always on its side, so that the wine remains in contact with the cork. This keeps the cork from drying out, shrinking and letting in air—a mortal enemy of wine.

PINOT GRIS
(*Pee*-no Gree)

REGION OR DISTRICT:
Willamette Valley (Wil-lam-ette Valley), northern Oregon.

COLOR:
Straw-yellow.

TASTE:
Touch of lemon; apples; spice; clean with crisp acidity and a clean finish.

WHEN TO DRINK:
Great years: 1–3 years (94, 92).
Good years: 1–2 years (93).

PRINCIPAL GRAPE:
Pinot Gris (*Pee*-no Gree).

BOUQUET:
Fruity; apple-like; scents of spice.

BEST CLUES:
Scent of apples with crisp acidity.

SERVE WITH:
Fish, shellfish, veal, light cream pastas, chicken.

SERVE AT:
50°–55°F.

NOTES: Oregon's reputation for Pinot Noir has somehow shunted into the background the fact that its wineries are now making exciting wines from the Pinot Gris grape which has a natural affinity to the soil and climate of the Willamette Valley. Interesting Pinot Gris' are being made by Adelsheim, Chehalem, Cooper Mountain, Cristom, Evesham Wood, Eyrie, Hinman, King Estate, Knudsen Erath, Lange, Montinore, Ponzi, Rex Hill, Silver Falls, Tyee and Yamhill Valley, to name but a hand-full. There is hardly a winemaker in Oregon that doesn't believe that the Pinot Gris has a great future there.

Q. Where is the Willamette Valley?
A. The Willamette Valley is Oregon's largest winegrowing region. It runs from the Columbia River in the north halfway down the state along the western border. Two other significant wine areas are in the Umpqua and Rogue Valleys.

CHARDONNAY
*(Shar-*doe-nay)

REGION OR DISTRICT:
Columbia Valley, Yakima Valley
and Walla-Walla Valley.

PRINCIPAL GRAPE:
Chardonnay *(Shar-*doe-nay).

BOUQUET:
Scents of apples; pears; tropical
fruit.

COLOR:
Straw-yellow.

TASTE:
Light to medium-bodied; touch
of oak; crisp citrus acidity.

BEST CLUES:
Scents of apples or pears. Crisp
finish.

WHEN TO DRINK:
Great years: 1–3 years (94, 91).
Good years: 1–2 years (93, 92).

SERVE WITH:
Seafood, fish, chicken, pork, veal.

SERVE AT:
50°–55°F.

NOTES: Washington State's growing reputation for outstanding Cabernet Sauvignons and Merlots has tended to obscure the fact that several of its Chardonnays could make it onto a list of "100 Best Chardonnays." They are leaner, less opulent than California Chardonnays with a crisp citrus acidity that goes well with seafood and white meats.

Some of the better Washington Chardonnays are produced by Arbor Crest, Bookwalter, Chateau Ste. Michelle, Columbia Crest, Columbia Winery, Covey Run, Facelli, Hogue, Kiona, L'Ecole No. 41, McCrea Cellars, Seth Ryan, Waterbrook, Washington Hills Cellars and Woodward Canyon.

Q. What is the second most planted white grape in Washington?
A. Riesling, and top producers are Arbor Crest Chateau Ste. Michelle, Columbia Crest, Columbia Winery, Covey Run, Hogue, Kiona, with Semillon steadily gaining in popularity.

Red Wine

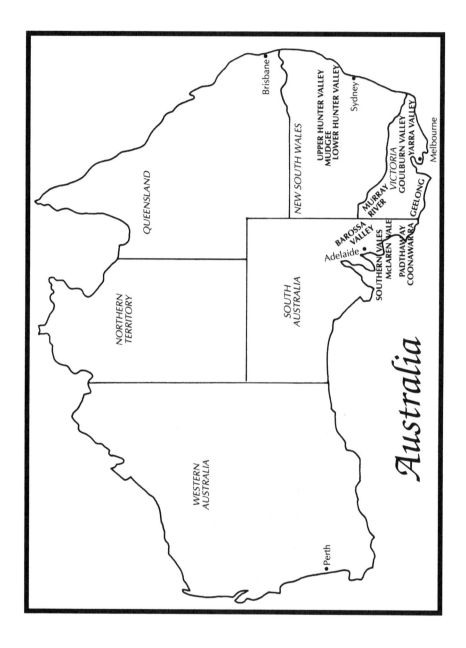

CABERNET SAUVIGNON
(Cab-air-*nay* So-veen-*yawn*)

REGION OR DISTRICT:
New South Wales; Victoria; South Australia.

PRINCIPAL GRAPE:
Cabernet Sauvignon (Cab-air-*nay* So-veen-*yawn*).

COLOR:
Medium to dark red.

BOUQUET:
Eucalyptus; mint; cassis; blackcurrants.

TASTE:
Rich hints of blackberry jam; chocolate; soft tannins.

BEST CLUES:
Mint; soft tannins.

WHEN TO DRINK:
Great years: 2–6 years (94, 90, 88, 87, 86).
Good years: 1–3 years (93, 92, 91).

SERVE WITH:
Lamb, beef, game, grilled or roast chicken, roast turkey, veal chops.

SERVE AT:
62°–68°F.

NOTES: Australia has three great wine regions: New South Wales with the best vineyards concentrated in the Lower Hunter Valley; Victoria with 12 vineyard regions surrounding Australia's second largest city, Melbourne; and Australia's largest wine producing district, South Australia, where seven wine regions stretch out from the city of Adelaide.

Western Australia is another wine region that is rapidly gaining a reputation for producing quality wines. Here the best vineyard regions surround the city of Perth and are: Lower Great Southern Region, Margaret River, Perth Hills, Southwest Coastal Plain and Swan Valley.

Australian Cabernets range in style from light to fairly full-bodied, although less full-bodied and less tannic than California Cabernets. They are also generally ready to drink sooner, within 3 to 6 years of their vintage.

Some well known producers are:

New South Wales: Lindemans, McWilliam's, Rothbury Estate, Saxonvale, Tyrrell's, Wyndham Estate.

Victoria: Brown Brothers, Chateau Tahbilk, Mitchelton, Preece, Taltarni, Tisdall.

South Australia: Black Opal, Chateau Reynella, Hardys, Henschke, Lindemans, Penfolds, Peter Lehmann, Roos Leap, Rosemount Estate, Seppelt, Wolf Blass, Yalumba.

Q. What is the most popular Australian quality red wine grape?
A. In less than forty years Cabernet Sauvignon has moved from almost non-existent to supremacy.

Q. Where in Australia does Cabernet Sauvignon excel?
A. In South Australia's Coonawarra, Barossa Valley and Southern Vales; in Central and Southern Victoria; and in the Lower Hunter Valley of New South Wales.

Q. Where are the best vineyards of New South Wales (NSW) located?
A. About a two-and-a-half hour drive north from Sidney brings you to the Lower Hunter Valley, where many of the best vineyards are located. The Upper Hunter Valley and Mudgee are the other important wine regions of New South Wales.

SHIRAZ
(Sear-*az*)

REGION OR DISTRICT:
New South Wales; Victoria; South Australia.

COLOR:
Medium to dark red.

TASTE:
Touch of pepper; suggestion of rich, black cherries; light to full-bodied; usually soft tannins.

WHEN TO DRINK:
Great years: 2–8 years depending on style (94, 90, 88, 87, 86).
Good years: 1–4 years (93, 92, 91, 89).

PRINCIPAL GRAPE:
Shiraz (Sear-*az*).

BOUQUET:
Black pepper; hint of mint; spice.

BEST CLUES:
Black pepper nose.

SERVE WITH:
Red meats, roast chicken, grilled veal chops, game.

SERVE AT:
65°–68°F.

NOTES: The Shiraz grape makes wines that vary in style from light to full-bodied and in taste from mediocre to great as evidenced by Penfolds' Grange Hermitage and Wolf Blass, both from the Barossa Valley in South Australia. The Shiraz (also called Hermitage) has a wine heritage of 150 years in New South Wales' Hunter Valley. The Shiraz blends well with Cabernet Sauvignon and it is common to see labels that proudly proclaim this dual heritage.

Well known Shiraz available in the United States are:

New South Wales: Arrowfield, Brokenwood, Lindemans, McWilliam's, Rosemount Estate, Rothbury Estate, Tyrrell's, Wyndham Estate.

Victoria: Brown Brothers, Campbells, Lindemans, Mitchelton, Seppelt Great Western, Redbank, Chateau Tahbilk, Taltarni, Tisdall.

South Australia: Chateau Reynella, Henschke, Kaiser Stuhl, Mildara, Penfolds, Peter Lehmann, Rosemount Estate, Ryecroft, Wynns Coonawarra Estate, Wolf Blass, Yalumba.

CABERNET SAUVIGNON
(Cab-air-*nay* So-veen-*yawn*)

REGION OR DISTRICT:
Mendoza and San Juan
Provinces, Argentina.

PRINCIPAL GRAPE:
Cabernet Sauvignon (Cab-air-*nay*
So-veen-*yawn*).

COLOR:
Light to medium red.

BOUQUET:
Hints of cedar; spice; cassis.

TASTE:
Soft, light tannins; medium-body
with a smooth aftertaste.

BEST CLUES:
Spicy nose redolent of a good
Bordeaux.

WHEN TO DRINK:
When purchased or within 4
years of the vintage.

SERVE WITH:
Red meats such as lamb,
steaks, roasts, hamburgers;
roast chicken, turkey.

SERVE AT:
62°–68°F.

NOTES: More than 70 percent of the more than 270 million cases of wine that are produced annually come from the province of Mendoza that runs along the foothills of the Andes Mountains bordering Chile. Another 20% of Argentina's wines are produced just to the north of Mendoza in the province of San Juan. Although a significant amount of rosé and white wine is produced, the red wines are the wines that excel.

Argentinian vineyards making the best red wines found in the United States are Humberto Canale, Caballero de la Cepa, Navarro Correas, Esmeralda, Etchart, Nicolas Fazio, Flichman, San Telmo, Pascual Tosco, Trapiche, and Bodega Weinert.

Q. What grape varietal in addition to Cabernet Sauvignon makes some of the best Argentinian red wines?
A. Malbec from vines originating in Bordeaux, but Merlot also makes some solid red wines.

CABERNET SAUVIGNON
(Cab-air-*nay* So-veen-*yawn*)

REGION OR DISTRICT:
Central zone near Santiago,
Chile in the Maipo Valley.

PRINCIPAL GRAPE:
Cabernet Sauvignon (Cab-air-*nay*
So-veen-*yawn*).

COLOR:
Medium red.

BOUQUET:
Hints of blackcurrants, cassis.

TASTE:
Light to medium-bodied; light
tannins.

BEST CLUES:
Hints of blackcurrants.

WHEN TO DRINK:
When released although a few
round out with 2 or 3 years extra
bottle age.

SERVE WITH:
Roast or grilled chicken and
turkey, red meats such as
hamburgers, steaks, lamb.

SERVE AT:
62°–68°F.

NOTES: Wines have been made in Chile for over 200 years. The best region is near Santiago in the central valley zone, bordered in the south by the Maipo River and the Aconcagua River in the north. Chilean wines are made from a full range of European varietals such as Cabernet Sauvignon, Chardonnay, Merlot, Pinot Noir, Sauvignon Blanc, Semillon, and Riesling.

Although Chilean white wines are improving, their best suit is in reds, especially Cabernet Sauvignon. Chilean Cabernets can be enjoyed as soon as they are released but a few round out and improve with a few additional years of bottle age. The standards are good and Chilean Cabernets can represent good value. The Maule Valley in southern Chile has a cooler climate and is developing a reputation for quality white wines.

Here are some of the better known Chilean wines found in the United States, all Cabernet Sauvignons: Canepa, Concha y Toro, Cousino Macul, Errázuriz-Panquehue, Los Vascos, Santa Carolina, Santa Rita, Miguel Torres, Traverso and Undurraga.

Burgundy

CHABLIS

•Dijon

Morey St. Denis ◦Gevrey-Chambertin
◦Chambolle-Musigny
COTE DE NUITS •Vougeot
Vosne-Romanée•
•Nuits-St.-Georges

•Aloxe-Corton

Beaune•
Volnay•Pommard
COTE DE BEAUNE
•Meursault
Puligny-Montrachet•
Chassagne-Montrachet•

Rully•
Mercurey•
Givry•
CHALONNAIS
•Chalon-sur-Saone

Saone R.

Tournus•

Lugny•
•Cluny
MACONNAIS
Pouilly-Fuissé•
•Macon

BEAUJOLAIS
St. Amour•
Julienas•
Chenas•
Moulin-a-Vent•
Fleurie•
Chiroubles•
Morgon•
Regnie•
Cote de Brouilly•
Brouilly•

Rhone R.

•Lyon

BEAUJOLAIS
(*Bo*-sjo-lay)

REGION OR DISTRICT:
Southern Burgundy.

COLOR:
Light to medium red with a
purple tinge.

TASTE:
Fruity and rich; medium dry with
touch of sweetness; refreshing
acidity; light in body.

WHEN TO DRINK:
Great years: 1–3 years (91).
Good years: 1–2 years (94, 93).
Poor years: (92).

PRINCIPAL GRAPE:
Gamay (Gam-ay) 100%.

BOUQUET:
Fragrant and very fruity; strawberries; often a suggestion of
sweetness on the palate.

BEST CLUES:
Suggestion of strawberries on the
nose.

SERVE WITH:
Goes with most food including
veal, chicken, pork, hamburger,
steak, pasta, grilled fish, grilled
shrimp and light to medium
seasoned foods.

SERVE AT:
55°–60°F.

NOTES: It has been reported that in every vintage more Beaujolais is
drunk in France alone than produced in Beaujolais. If this is so, then
much of what is shipped and sold as Beaujolais is not Beaujolais, although it might be a pleasant wine. To avoid any deception you will do
well to buy only wines labeled "Beaujolais-Village" from a reputable
shipper or a wine of one of ten communes that use their own names
and are known as "Beaujolais Crus": Côte-de-Brouilly (Coat-duh-*Brew*-
yee), Brouilly (*Brew*-yee), Chénas (*Shay*-nah), Chiroubles (Sheer-roubl),
Fleurie (*Flur*-ree), Juliénas (Jule-*yea-nahss*), Morgon (Mor-*gawn*), Moulin-
à-Vent (Moo-*lawn*-ah-von), Regnié (*Rain*-yea) and St.-Amour (Sant-ah-
moor). Moulin-à-Vent is generally conceded to be the most full-bodied.
These are the top growths of Beaujolais and are held to higher standards

under the Appellation Contrôlée laws. They are a bit more expensive, but the added value in taste is usually worth the difference in price.

Beaujolais is the largest district in the Burgundy region and the most beautiful. The allure of Beaujolais wines is their simplicity, their fruity freshness and ease of drinking with almost any food.

Consistently fine Beaujolais shippers are Chateau de La Chaize, Georges Duboeuf, Joseph Drouhin, Sylvain Fessy, Louis Jadot, Louis Latour, Paul Sapin, Robert Sarrau, Pasquier-Desvignes, Mommessin, and Jean-Marc Aujoux.

Q. Are the wines of Beaujolais 100% red?
A. Almost but not quite, about 1% being white. The best Beaujolais Blanc is made from the Chardonnay grape.

Q. What is the average annual production of Beaujolais?
A. About 14.5 million cases of which about one-third is Nouveau, one-third Crus and one-third Beaujolais-Villages and plain Beaujolais.

Q. What is Beaujolais Nouveau?
A. As soon as the grapes are harvested (usually in September or early October), they are put into vats and their own weight crushes the bottom grapes and fermentation begins. After fermentation is finished, it is bottled and released on the third Thursday in November following the harvest. It is a wine to drink as soon as it is released.

BURGUNDY or BOURGOGNE
(Bor-*goan*-yuh)

REGION OR DISTRICT:
Burgundy, Central-Eastern France.

COLOR:
Light to medium red; brown or orange rim indicates has reached or passed maturity.

TASTE:
Somewhat tannic when young; tannin smooths out with maturity. Dry and soft with the suggestion of sweetness on the palate and finish. Medium-bodied.

WHEN TO DRINK:
Great years: 3–12 years (90, 89, 85).
Good years: 1–5 years (93, 91, 92, 88, 87).
Poor years: (94, 86).

PRINCIPAL GRAPE:
Pinot Noir (*Pee*-no *Nwahr*) 100%.

BOUQUET:
Earthy; suggestive of boiled cabbage; roasting coffee; prunes; plums.

BEST CLUES:
A hint of boiled cabbage in the smell.

SERVE WITH:
Game, roast duck or goose, pheasant, beef, lamb, veal, cheese, grilled and baked scallops, tuna, swordfish.

SERVE AT:
62°–68°F.

NOTES: Much red wine is sold under the Burgundy label that doesn't smell or taste of the Pinot Noir grape. Therefore it is essential that you know the reputation the shipper or négociant before buying red Burgundies.

Here are some producers to look for: Clair-Dau, Comte Georges de Vogué, Domaine Dujac, Jean Grivot, Jean Gros, Daniel Rion, Domaine de la Romanée-Conti, Henri Jayer, Joseph Drouhin, Joseph Faiveley, Louis Jadot, Louis Latour, Maison Leroy, Mongeard-Mugneret, Pierre Gelin, Remoissenet and Armand Rousseau. An old French proverb tells us that "There is no sounder purchase for a tired and depressed man than a bottle of good Burgundy."

Q. What is a Grand Cru vineyard?
A. Grand Cru means "great growth" and these vineyards are entitled to use this designation on their labels. A number of these vineyards are owned by many owners as in the case of Clos de Vougeot (over 70 owners) and Chambertin (over 25 owners). Consequently, these multi-owned Grand Cru vineyards produce wines with variations in quality.

Q. What is a Premier Cru vineyard?
A. Premier Cru means first growth, and by tradition (but not always by taste) they are considered a slight step down in quality from Grand Cru wines.

Q. What is the Côte de Nuits?
A. The Côte de Nuits is the northern region of the Côte d'Or that produces all (except for one: Corton) of the Grand Cru or great growth red Burgundies. It begins in the north below Dijon and ends just before Aloxe-Corton.

Q. What makes up the wine districts known as Burgundy?
A. Burgundy is an area that begins 70 miles southeast of Paris in Chablis and ends near Lyons, a distance of 225 miles. There are five major districts: Chablis in the north; Côte d'Or (consisting of the Côte de Nuits in the north and the Côte de Beaune in the south); Côte Chalonnaise; Maconnais; and Beaujolais. Pinot Noir grapes make all the great red Burgundies; Chardonnay all the great whites.

Q. Where is and what is Beaune?
A. Beaune is a town located in the middle of the Côte d'Or where many wine producers and shippers have their offices. It has been the wine center of Burgundy for hundreds of years. The famous Hospices de Beaune wine auction is held here every November. It is an interesting old town and worth a special visit.

Q. Where is the Côte Chalonnais and what are its best known wines?
A. The Côte Chalonnais begins just south of the village of Chassagne-Montrachet. Its vineyards surround the towns of Givry (Shev-*ree*), Mercurey (Mair-coor-*ay*), Mantagny (Mawn-tan-*yee*), Rully (Roo-*ye*) and produce quality red and white wines from the Pinot Noir and Chardonnay grapes.

Q. Does Burgundy have an equivalent of Bordeaux chateau bottling, *Mise en Bouteille au Chateau?*

A. Yes. In Burgundy when the wine has been bottled at the vineyard by the producer, the label will read *Mise à la Propriété* or *Mise en Bouteille au Domaine* or *Mise au Domaine.*

Q. How are the wines of Burgundy classified?

A. The most distinguished (but not always the best) are labeled Grand Cru and are identified by their vineyard names, such as Chambertin, Romaneé-Conti, Clos de Vougeot, Montrachet, Musigny, etc. There are 37 such Grands Crus Burgundy wines both red and white, seven of which are in Chablis. Burgundy wines of a slightly less pedigree are labeled Premiers Crus. Next comes appellation village wines such as Chassagne-Montrachet, Macon Village, Nuits St. Georges, etc. and lastly, wines from generic viticultural regions.

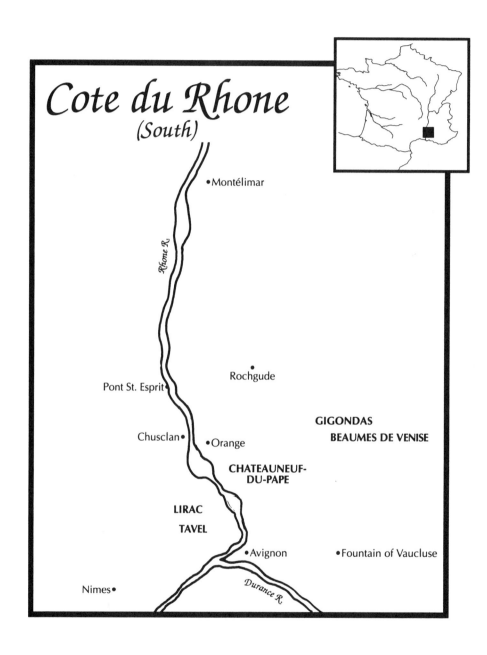

Cote du Rhone
(South)

CHATEAUNEUF-DU-PAPE
(Shat-toe-*nuff* dew *Pahp*)

REGION OR DISTRICT:
Southern Rhône.

PRINCIPAL GRAPE:
Grenache (Grah-*nahsh*).

COLOR:
Deep reddish-purple when young; dark red with maturity; heavy "legs"; brown rim indicates considerable age.

BOUQUET:
Earthy; black pepper; plummy; spicy with a suggestion of sweetness; alcoholic; coffee-like with considerable age.

TASTE:
Robust and full-bodied; peppery; chocolate richness; alcoholic; fruity and rich; light to medium tannins; dry with a full aftertaste.

SERVE WITH:
All red meats, spicy foods, roast chicken, roast duck, pastas with red sauces.

SERVE AT:
62°–68°F.

WHEN TO DRINK:
Great years: 3–12 years (90, 89, 88, 86, 85).
Good years: 2–5 years (94, 92, 86, 84, 83).
Poor years: (93, 91, 87).

NOTES: Under existing laws, Châteauneuf-du-Pape can be a blend of as many as 13 grape varieties with Grenache usually the chief grape. No other great wine producing region in the world (except Port) allows such a large number of grapes. Châteauneuf-du-Pape has the highest (12½%) minimum alcohol strength of any French wine. It can usually be drunk after 3 years, but in good to great vintages improves with further bottle age. Old Châteauneuf-du-Papes from excellent vintages can be superb.

Some of the best vineyards or producers include Château de Beaucastel, La Bernardine, Bosquet des Papes, Brunel-Les Cailloux, Les Cèdres, Clos du Caillou, Clos du Mont-Olivet, Clos des Papes, Pignan, Chateau Fines des Roches, Chateau Fortia, Château de la Gardine, Domaine de la Janasse, Château Mont-Redon, Château de la Nerthe, Château Rayas, Cuvée du Vatican, Domaine Pontifical, Domaine de la Roquette, Domaine de la Solitude, Le Vieux Donjon, Domaine du Vieux Télégraphe.

Q. How did Châteauneuf-du-Pape get its name?
A. In the 14th century Pope Clement V moved the Papacy from Rome to Avignon. Ten miles north of Avignon he built his papal summer residency, Châteauneuf-du-Pape.

Q. How many grape varieties are permitted to make Châteauneuf-du-Pape?
A. Thirteen, but few producers use that number. The four principal grapes used are: Grenache, Syrah, Mourvèdre and Cinsault.

Q. What is sediment?
A. Most fine wines, especially wines older then 5 or 6 years, throw a sediment or deposit in the bottle. This sediment is nothing more than the result of the wine's development and, hopefully, improvement. It is not only normal but desirable.

Q. Why should the sediment be removed before drinking the wine?
A. If the sediment becomes mixed in with the wine before drinking, it will affect the wine's taste, making it harsh and bitter. It also looks terrible floating in the glass.

Q. How do you remove the sediment?
A. Stand the bottle upright for several hours (preferably a day or so) before drinking to allow the sediment to collect at the bottom of the bottle. Then over a light (a candle or a light bulb, after removing the shade from a lamp), carefully pour the wine into a clean decanter. When the sediment appears in the neck of the wine bottle, stop pouring, and you will have a clear, sediment-free bottle of wine.

CORNAS
(Kor-*nass*)

REGION OR DISTRICT:
Northern Rhône.

PRINCIPAL GRAPE:
Syrah (Seer-*rah*).

COLOR:
Dark red; ruby.

BOUQUET:
Often closed but with proper bottle age develops overtones of raspberries; pepper; spice.

TASTE:
Full-bodied and tannic with a long-lasting but slightly bitter finish.

BEST CLUES:
Spicy bouquet with hints of raspberrries.

WHEN TO DRINK:
Great years: 4–12 years (90, 89, 88, 85).
Good years: 2–5 years (94, 93, 91).
Poor years: (92).

SERVE WITH:
Red meats and game.

SERVE AT:
62°–68°F.

NOTES: The town of Cornas is located on the west bank of the Rhône River (on your right as you travel south) about 12 miles south of Hermitage. These are big tannic wines that resemble in power but not in finesse Hermitage and need considerable bottle age to reach maturity. Although they do not develop the elegance of Hermitages, when mature and drunk with rich, hardy foods, they can be superb. Since they are less expensive than Hermitage, they are usually excellent value.

Some well-known producers are: Guy de Barjac, Thierry Allemand, Chapoutier, Auguste Clape, Jean-Luc Colombo, Domaine Jean Lionnet, Paul Etienne, Paul Jaboulet Aîné, Marcel Juge, Robert Michel, Noel Verset, Vidal-Fleury and Alain Voge.

Q. How large are the vineyards of Cornas?
A. There are only about 130 acres of vines planted in Cornas so it is not exactly a household word, but a wine worth getting to know.

CÔTE DU RHÔNE
(Coat-dew-Rhône)

CÔTE DU RHÔNE VILLAGE
(Coat-dew-Rhône Vee-*lage*)

REGION OR DISTRICT:
Rhône Valley.

PRINCIPAL GRAPE:
Varied.

COLOR:
Red, white and rosé but usually red.

BOUQUET:
A variety of aromas and bouquets.

BEST CLUES:
Varied.

TASTE:
A variety of tastes.

SERVE WITH:
Depends on whether it is red, white or rosé.

WHEN TO DRINK:
Normally within 1 to 3 years of the vintage.

SERVE AT:
62°–68°F.

NOTES: The Côte du Rhône is a long narrow stretch that borders both sides of the Rhône River beginning below Vienne in the north at Côte Rotie and ending 140 miles south at Avignon. Côte du Rhônes vary in quality but often represent excellent value. Another appellation is Côte du Rhône Village. These wines are usually red and generally a little higher in quality than generic Côte du Rhône wines.

Here are some good producers of Côte du Rhônes and Côte du Rhône Villages: Paul Autard, André Brunel, Daniel Brusset, Les Cailloux, Chateau des Tours, Domaine des Armouriers Villages, Domaine de Beaurenard, Domaine des Moulins, Domaine de la Mordorée, Domaine Pelequié, Domaine de la Renjarde, Domaine Sâinte-Anne, Domaine La Soumade, Domaine de Vieux Chene, Paul Jaboulet Aine, Georges Duboeuf, Vidal-Fluery, J. M. Gerin, E. Guigal, Jacques Reynaud and La Vieille Ferme.

CÔTE RÔTIE
(Coat Ro-*tee*)

REGION OR DISTRICT:
Northern Rhône.

COLOR:
Deep ruby with purple tinge
when young; dark red with
maturity; heavy "legs."

TASTE:
Raspberries; blackcurrant fruit;
fruity with spicy or peppery overtones; full-bodied with balanced
acidity and tannin; dry aftertaste.

WHEN TO DRINK:
Great years: 4–20 years (91, 90,
89, 88, 85, 83, 78).
Good years: 2–7 years (94, 93, 92,
87, 86).
Poor years: (84).

PRINCIPAL GRAPE:
Syrah (Seer-*rah*).

BOUQUET:
Raspberry-like; peppery; cassis;
dried orange skins; rich and
fruity.

SERVE WITH:
Beef, lamb, roast chicken, roast
or grilled veal, cheese.

SERVE AT:
62°–68°F.

NOTES: About 22 miles south of Lyons at Ampuis the vineyards of the
Rhône begin at Côte Rôtie (roasted slope). Some of the world's finest
wines come from the Syrah grapes that grow on these steep granitic
hillsides overlooking the Rhône River. Côte Rôties develop complexi-
ties and nuances of bouquets and flavors that only the world's great
wines achieve. Although mothered by the same grape as red Hermitage, there are subtle differences in taste between these two great wines:
delicacy and finesse in the Côte Rôties; assertiveness and body in the
Hermitages. Both should be an integral part of any serious wine cellar.
Hot summers along the Rhône are the rule, and there are more consistently good years than in most other wine districts in France, and mature and well-made Côte Rôties and Hermitages rival in quality and
complexity the best red Burgundies and Bordeaux. Because Côte Rôties

and Hermitages are rarely château or domaine bottled, you must be especially careful of the name behind the bottle.

Some of the principal producers of quality Côte Rôties are: Gilles and Pierre Barge, Bernard Burgaud, M. Chapoutier, René Clusel, Vidal-Fleury, Delas Frères, Henri Gallet, Albert Gerin, Gentaz-Dervieux, E. Guigal, Paul Jaboulet Aîné, Jean-Paul and Jean-Luc Jamet, Robert Jasmin, Michel Ogier, René Rostaing, and Vallouit.

Q. Are any sparkling wines made in the Northern Rhône wine regions?
A. Yes. Just to the south of Cornas is the little town of St. Péray where a sparkling wine is made in the Champagne method from the Marsanne and Roussanne grapes.

GIGONDAS
(*She*-gone-das)

REGION OR DISTRICT:
Southern Rhône.

COLOR:
Deep ruby red when young with
purple-blue tints.

TASTE:
Full-bodied, robust, tannic when
young, long finish.

WHEN TO DRINK:
Great years: 4–12 years (90, 89,
88, 86, 85).
Good years: 2–5 years (94, 92).
Poor years: (93, 91, 87).

PRINCIPAL GRAPE:
Grenache (Grah-*nahsh*).

BOUQUET:
Spices; pepper; licorice;
raspberries.

BEST CLUES:
Spice; pepper.

SERVE WITH:
Red meats, roast chicken, game.

SERVE AT:
62°–68°F.

NOTES: Although Gigondas shares similarities in taste with its more famous neighbor, Châteauneuf-du-Pape, it is normally a bigger, sturdier wine with lots of fruit. It can be drunk young but gains immeasurably after 4 or 5 years from its vintage date. In outstanding vintages it needs 5 years or more of bottle age to be drinking at its best. It never tastes better than when accompanying a steak, leg of lamb or highly seasoned food.

The following is a list of well-known producers: Daniel Brusset, Edmunde Burle, Domaine du Cayron, Roger Combe, Michel Faraud, Delas Frères, Domaine de Font-Sane, E. Moulin de la Gardette, Domaine Les Goubert, Domaine du Gour de Chaulé, E. Guigal, Château de Montmirail, Domaine des Pesquiers, Chateau Raspail Ay, Domaine de Saint-Gayan, Domaine Santa-Duc.

Q. Who is Bacchus?
A. In Roman mythology, Bacchus is the God of wine.

GRAVES
(Grahv)

REGION OR DISTRICT:
Southwest of Bordeaux.

COLOR:
Medium to dark red; brown rim indicates reaching or passing maturity.

TASTE:
Dry; mouth-puckering when young; tannin precipitates; fruity; rich flavors with a smooth after-taste.

WHEN TO DRINK:
Great years: 5–20 years (90, 89, 88, 83, 82, 78, 70).
Good years: 3–10 years (94, 88, 86, 85).
Poor years: (93, 92, 91, 87).

PRINCIPAL GRAPE:
Cabernet Sauvignon (Cab-air-*nay* So-veen-*yawn*).

BOUQUET:
Cedar; dry tea leaves; black-currants; tobacco; vanilla.

BEST CLUES:
Cedarwood bouquet with hints of a cigar box.

SERVE WITH:
Lamb, beef, game, cheese.

SERVE AT:
62°–65°F.

NOTES: The best wines of Graves come from vineyards in the northern appellation of "Pessac-Léognan" where the great vineyards of Chateau Haut-Brion, La Mission Haut-Brion, Haut-Bailly, Pape Clément, de Fieu-zal, La Tour Martillac and Domaine de Chevalier are located. Red Graves have many of the same taste and bouquet characteristics of their north-ern Médoc neighbors but with a slightly earthier character.

Except for La Mission Haut-Brion and Haut-Bailly, all of the above vineyards produce some white wines.

Q. What are some other reliable Graves chateaux producing quality red wines?
A. Chateaux Chantegrive, Cruzeau, La Louviere, Rochemorin.

HERMITAGE
(Air-mee-*taj*)

REGION OR DISTRICT:
Northern Rhône at Tain.

PRINCIPAL GRAPE:
Syrah (Seer-*rah*).

COLOR:
Deep ruby with purple tinge
when young; dark red with
maturity; heavy "legs."

BOUQUET:
Raspberry-like; peppery; cassis;
dried orange skins; rich and
fruity.

TASTE:
Raspberries; blackcurrant fruit;
fruity with spicy or peppery overtones; full-bodied with balanced
acidity and tannin; dry aftertaste.

SERVE WITH:
Beef, lamb, roast chicken, roast
or grilled veal, cheese.

SERVE AT:
62°–68°F.

WHEN TO DRINK:
Great years: 5–20 years (91, 90,
89, 88, 85, 83, 78).
Good years: 2–8 years (94, 93, 92,
87, 86).
Poor years: (84).

NOTES: Hermitage [see Côte Rôtie at page 85] and the neighboring vineyards of Crozes-Hermitage are the only significant vineyards
located on the East Bank of the Rhône. The Crozes-Hermitage vineyards surround Hermitage on three sides with the town of Tain and the
Rhône River to the west. The wines of Crozes-Hermitage have many of
Hermitage's characteristics but exhibit less power, finesse, concentration, and bouquet. Still, they are quality wines of good value. Crozes-
Hermitage matures earlier and is ready to drink a little sooner than
Hermitage.

Some of the better known producers of Hermitage are: M. Chapoutier, Gérard Chave, Jean-Louis Chave, Delas Frères, J. L. Grippat, E.
Guigal, Paul Jaboulet Aîné, and H. Sorrel.

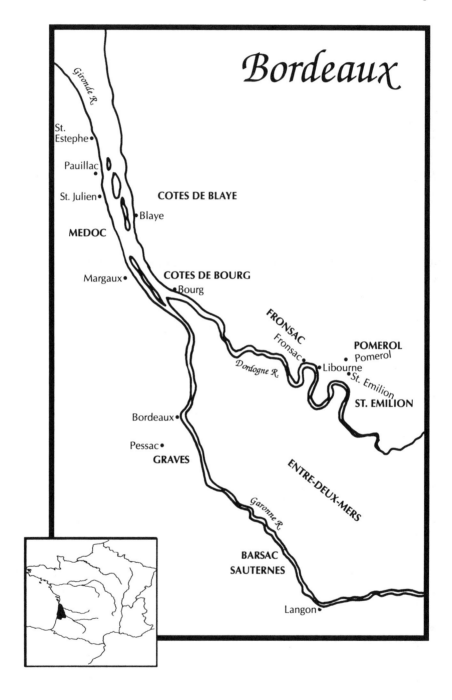

MÉDOC
(*May*-dock)

REGION OR DISTRICT:
North of Bordeaux.

COLOR:
Medium to dark red; brown rim indicates reaching or passing maturity.

TASTE:
Dry; mouth-puckering when young; tannin precipitates, and develops rich flavors with a smooth aftertaste.

WHEN TO DRINK:
Great years: 5–20 years (90, 89, 88, 85, 78, 70).
Good years: 3–10 years (94, 86, 83).
Poor years: (93, 92, 91, 87).

PRINCIPAL GRAPE:
Cabernet Sauvignon (Cab-air-*nay* So-veen-*yawn*).

BOUQUET:
Cedar; dry tea leaves; black-currants; tobacco; vanilla.

BEST CLUES:
Cedarwood bouquet; some compare it to the smell of a cigar box.

SERVE WITH:
Lamb, beef, game, roast fowl such as duck, goose, partridge, pheasant, grilled veal chops, cheese.

SERVE AT:
62°–65°F.

NOTES: If both quality and quantity are considered, the Médoc is the world's greatest wine producing region. Here, as in Graves, the primary grape is the Cabernet Sauvignon, which produces hard, tannic wines when young but, given proper bottle age, wines that develop incredible complexity and taste. In great vintages the best Médocs usually need 10 or more years to reach their full potential. They are not wines for the impatient. When at their best they reach heights that only a few other wines can climb. The Graves district produces two such rivals, Château Haut-Brion and La Mission Haut-Brion. Recent enormous price increases of classified Médocs will put them out of the reach of many wine lovers. But for that special occasion 10 or so years from now, stock in a few bottles of 1990, 89, and 82. For those who don't want to pay the price for a classified growth, consistently excellent wines are made by such non-classified châteaux as Beaumont, Beau-Site, Chasse-Spleen, Cissac, Citran, Haut-Marbuzet, Lanessan, Loudenne, Meyney, Les Ormes-de-Pez, de Pez, Phélan-Ségur, Sociando-Mallet, La Lagune, La Tour-de-Mons, and others.

Q. What are the four famous communes of the Médoc?
A. St. Estèphe, Pauillac, St. Julien and Margaux.

Q. What are the two most famous wines of St. Estèphe, the northern-most commune of the Médoc?
A. Cos d'Estournel and Montrose. Other high quality wines from this commune are Chateaux Calon-Ségur, Lafon-Rochet, Cos Labory, de Pez, Beau-Site, Meyney, Les Ormes-de-Pez, Phélan Ségur, Capbern-Gasqueton, and Haut-Marbuzet.

Q. What are the most famous wines of Pauillac?
A. Lafite-Rothschild, Latour and Mouton-Rothschild followed by Pichon-Longueville-Lalande, Pichon-Longueville Baron and Lynch-Bages.

Q. What are the most outstanding wines of St. Julien?
A. Léoville-Las-Cases, Ducru-Beaucaillou, Gruaud-Larose, LaGrange, Léoville-Barton, Léoville-Poyferré, Beychevelle, Branaire-Ducru, Lagrange, Langoa Barton and Talbot.

Q. Does the commune of Margaux make wines that rival those of Pauillac, St. Julien and St. Estèphe?
A. Yes. Margaux wines are probably the most delicate, perfumed wines of the Médoc. The clear leader is Chateau Margaux followed by Chateaux Palmer, Lascombes, Rausan-Ségla (a favorite wine of Thomas Jefferson), d' Issan, Durfort-Vivens, Giscours, Kirwan and Prieure-Lichine.

Q. What is the classification of 1855?
A. During the Paris Exhibition of 1855 Bordeaux wine merchants were asked to classify the wines of the Médoc and Sauternes. They submitted a list of 61 Chateaux classified First through Fifth Growths, all from the Médoc except for Haut-Brion and 22 Sauternes. These rankings were based on the prices the wines had sold for over many years. The list was officially accepted by the French government and persists to this day with only one change: in 1973 Chateau Mouton-Rothschild was elevated to a First Growth.

POMEROL
(Paum-ma-rawl)

REGION OR DISTRICT:
East of Bordeaux.

COLOR:
Light to dark red; brown rim indicates reaching or passing maturity.

TASTE:
Dry; tannic and astringent when young; fruity; rich and smooth when mature.

WHEN TO DRINK:
Great years: 5–15 years (90, 89, 88, 85, 82).
Good years: 2–6 years (94, 91, 87, 86).
Poor years: (93, 92).

PRINCIPAL GRAPE:
Merlot (Mair-low).

BOUQUET:
Cedarwood, but less pronounced than with Médocs; blackcurrants; plummy.

BEST CLUES:
Cedarwood, blackcurrant or plummy bouquet.

SERVE WITH:
Beef, game, pheasant, lamb, cheese.

SERVE AT:
62°–68°F.

NOTES: This is the Bordeaux appellation that produces the world's most expensive wine—Chateau Pétrus. Tiny in size, Pomerol has never been officially classified but then it doesn't need it. If the bottle label says "Appellation Pomerol Contrôlée" and is from a good vintage, you have every reason to expect that the quality of the wine is quite good. Unfortunately, the wine-world has discovered the high quality of Pomerol wines, and as a group they are Bordeaux's most expensive wines. Here are some Pomerols of breed and elegance: Certan de May, La Conseillante, La Croix de Gay, L'Église-Clinet, L'Évangile, La Fleur de Gay, La Fleur-Pétrus, Latour àPomerol, Petit-Village, Le Pin, Clos René, Trotanoy, Vieux Château Certan, but there are many others.

Q. How expensive is Chateau Pétrus and why is it so expensive?

A. It is the most expensive red wine in the world. Why? First, year in and year out, Pétrus makes world class wines. Second, its production is very small, and so the principle of supply and demand takes over. And third, exaccerbating the normal forces of supply and demand is what I call the "in" factor. Pétrus is an "in" wine, and millionaires throughout the world "must" have it.

Q. How big a vineyard area is Pomerol?

A. Pomerol consists of 1,850 acres of vines with about 180 estates making 300,000 cases. These vineyard estates are so small that only twenty or so properties have 25 or more acres of vineyards.

Q. What is the principal grape varietal of Pomerol?

A. 70% of the vines are Merlot.

Q. The words "Lalande de Pomerol" on a label means what?

A. It means that the wine comes from the commune of Lalande de Pomerol that lies to the north of Pomerol, and though these wines can be quite nice, they are not of the same high quality as those designated "Pomerol."

Q. Why are the wines of Pomerol and St. Émilion sometimes referred to as the "Burgundies of Bordeaux"?

A. Because they are softer and generally earlier maturing than their dryer and more austere Médoc and Graves neighbors.

ST.-ÉMILION
(San-tay *Mee*-lee-awn)

REGION OR DISTRICT:
East of Bordeaux.

COLOR:
Light to dark red; brown rim indicates reaching or has reached maturity.

TASTE:
Dry; tannic and astringent when young; fruity, rich and smooth when mature.

WHEN TO DRINK:
Great years: 5–15 years (90, 89, 88, 85, 82).
Good years: 3–7 years (94, 91, 86).
Poor years: (93, 92).

PRINCIPAL GRAPE:
Cabernet Franc (Cab-air-*nay Frawnc*) and Merlot (Mair-low).

BOUQUET:
A whiff of cedarwood, but less pronounced than with Médocs; blackcurrants; plummy.

BEST CLUES:
Cedarwood, blackcurrant or plummy bouquet.

SERVE WITH:
Beef, game, stews, cheese, lamb, veal chops.

SERVE AT:
62°–68°F.

NOTES: The quaint town of St.-Émilion is about 25 miles northeast of Bordeaux on the east side of the Gironde River. The wines of St.-Émilion are less tannic than Médocs, and are usually ready to drink sooner than most Médocs yet have a superb ability to age in the bottle.

The vineyards of St.-Émilion consist of two separate districts, the Côtes and the Graves. Clustered on hillsides and plains surrounding the town are a number of its most famous vineyards: Chateaux L'Arrosée, Ausone, Beauséjour, Belair, Canon, Clos Fourtet, Fonplégade, La Gaffelière, Magdelaine, Troplong-Mondot, Pavie, and Trottevieille. Further to the northwest and toward Pomerol is the Graves area (gravel soil) and it is here that St.-Émilion's greatest wine is made—Chateau Cheval Blanc (White Horse). Other famous vineyards from this area are Chateaux La Dominique, Figeac (Fee-jack), La Tour Figeac, La Tour du Pin-Figeac, and Ripeau.

Q. What is the oldest wine town in France?

A. St.-Émilion stands in a cluster of hills two miles from the right bank of the Dordogne River near Libourne. When in the Bordeaux area St.-Émilion is worth a special visit and, if time permits, an overnight stay.

Q. Are any of the surrounding communes entitled to add "St.-Émilion" to their labels?

A. Yes. There are six surrounding communes entitled to add St.-Émilion as a suffix to their appellations. They are Lussac St.-Émilion, Montagne St.-Émilion, Parsac St.-Émilion, Puisseguin St.-Émilion, Sables St.-Émilion, and St. Georges St.-Émilion. Although most of the wines from these communes are good both in taste and value, they should not be confused with the generally higher quality wines that carry the plain appellation "St.-Émilion."

Q. In evaluating the quality of a wine, is the vintage important?

A. The vintage or date when the grapes were harvested and the wine was made is important in determining a wine's quality.

Q. Should all wines be decanted?

A. No, but most young wines improve by being allowed to breathe for an hour or so. Aeration, or allowing the wine to "breathe," allows the bouquet to develop. Old red wines need special treatment, and here experience is your best guide. For red wines 5–10 years of age, decant the wine about 2 hours before serving and leave the neck of the decanter open. For older wines, decant about an hour before serving and put a stopper in the decanter. For wines 20 or more years old decant and serve.

ST. JOSEPH
(Sant Sho-*zef*)

REGION OR DISTRICT:
Northern Rhône, across the river
from Hermitage.

COLOR:
Light red to ruby when young
with tinges of brown with age.

TASTE:
A slight touch of licorice; dry,
rich and fruity with a slightly
bitter finish.

WHEN TO DRINK:
Great years: 3–7 years (91, 90,
89, 88).
Good years: 1–4 years (94, 93, 92).

PRINCIPAL GRAPE:
Syrah (Seer-*rah*).

BOUQUET:
Pepper, raspberries.

BEST CLUES:
Pepper and raspberries on the
nose.

SERVE WITH:
Grilled chicken, red meats, veal
chops, game.

SERVE AT:
62°–65°F.

NOTES: St. Joseph is opposite Hermitage on the west bank of the Rhône. Although made from the Syrah grape, it is lighter than its famous neighbor. There have been recent extensive plantings of the St. Joseph vineyards and these wines can exhibit a considerable difference in the quality. At their best they are packed with fruit and easy to drink when young, but with a spine of tannin that adds to their enjoyment and allows them to improve with some bottle age. Still, they should be drunk relatively young.

The following is a list of reliable shippers: M. Chapoutier's "Deschants," J. L. Chave, Pascal Perrier's "Domaine de Gachon," André Perret's "Les Grisieres," Pierre Gaillard, Alain Graillot, Bernard Gripa, Jean-Louis Grippat, Clos de L'Arbalestrier, Pierre Coursodon, Domaine du Chêne, Maurice Courbis, Domaine de Fauterie, Vidal-Fleury, Paul Jaboulet Aîné's "Le Grand Pompée."

TAVEL
(Tah-*vel*)

REGION OR DISTRICT:
Southern Rhône on the opposite
bank of the Rhône River from
Châteauneuf-du-Pape and
Gigondas.

COLOR:
Rosé or salmon pink.

TASTE:
Spicy, dry and surprisingly
alcoholic with more body than
is usually associated with rosés.
Balanced acidity.

WHEN TO DRINK:
Great and good years: 1–3 years
(94, 92).
Poor years: (93, 91).

PRINCIPAL GRAPE:
Grenache (Gren-*ahsh*).

BOUQUET:
Flowery; fruity.

BEST CLUES:
Fruity bouquet; full-bodied.

SERVE WITH:
White meats, fish, Oriental
foods such as Chinese, Thai
and Japanese.

SERVE AT:
45°–50°F.

NOTES: Tavel has the reputation for making some of the best rosé wines in the world. It is surprisingly high in alcohol, often reaching 13 to 14%. Like all rosés, Tavel is a wine to be drunk young while still fresh, crisp and fruity. Although AOC laws allow as many as nine grapes, Grenache, Clairette and Cinsault are the three most important.

Some of the best Tavels are produced by: Château d'Aquéria, Chateau de Manissy, Chateau de Trinquevedel, Domaine Maby La Forcadière, Domaine De La Génestière, Domaine de Montezarques, Domaine de la Mordorée, Delas Frères, E. Guigal, Les Vignerons de Tavel, Le Vieux Moulin.

Lirac, Bandol, Bellet, in southern France, and Anjou from vineyards along the Loire River are other areas producing high quality rosés.

BAROLO
(Bar-*o*-low)

REGION OR DISTRICT:
Piedmont, northwest Italy.

PRINCIPAL GRAPE:
Nebbiolo (Neb-be-*o*-low) 100%.

COLOR:
Dark red; heavy "legs"; browns
and develops orange rim with
age.

BOUQUET:
Earthy and pungent; leather;
smokey; tar; suggestion of
mushrooms; licorice.

TASTE:
Tannic and acidic when young;
dry and rich with age; medium to
full-bodied; bitter aftertaste.

BEST CLUES:
Bitter aftertaste.

SERVE WITH:
Rich pastas, stews, red meats,
game, gorgonzola (or any blue
veined) cheese.

WHEN TO DRINK:
Great years: 3–12 years from
vintage (90, 89, 88, 85, 82).
Good years: 3–6 years from
vintage (94, 87, 86).
Poor years: (93, 92, 91, 84).

SERVE AT:
62°–68°F.

NOTES: In the northwest corner of Italy, the Piedmont produces three
of that country's finest wines: Barolo, Barbaresco (Bar-bear-esk-o) and
Gattinara (Ghatt-een-ah-rah). Barolo is considered by many wine connoisseurs as Italy's greatest wine. It is aged in casks for 2 or more years
and has a capacity for further aging in the bottle. Its high alcohol
(13%–15%) is normally detectable on the nose. Barolos should be decanted 2 to 3 hours before drinking. Although less full-bodied, Barbarescos and Gattinaras need bottle age to develop their full potential.

Some well-known producers of both Barolos and Barbarescos are:
Marchesi di Barolo, Bruno Ceretto, Pio Cesare, Michele Chiarlo, Fon-
tanafredda, Angelo Gaja, Bruno Giacosa, Giuseppe Mascarello, Fratelli
Oddero, Alfredo Prunotto, Renato Ratti, Scarpa, Vietti.

Quality producers of Barolos are: Elio Altare, Batasiolo, Bersano,
Giacomo Borgogno, Clerico, Bel Colle, Aldo Conterno, Giacomo Con-

terno, Gianni Gagliardo, Granduca, Marcarini, Bartolo Mascarello, Giuseppe Rinaldi, Luciano Sandrone, Paolo Scavino, Roberto Voerzio.

Some well regarded producers of Barbarescos are: Luigi Bianco, Fratelli Cigliuti, Punset, Secondo Pasquero Elia, Produttori del Barbaresco, Le Colline, Giuseppe Cortese, Castello di Neive, Marcorino, Marchesi di Gresy and Moccagatta.

Q. Why are so many Barolos and Barbarescos disappointing?
A. Because they are drunk too old. Most of these wines can't handle the extended bottle age (15–20 or more years) that many wine writers and vintners recommend. It is far better to drink a wine when it's a little too tannic but full of fruit than when it is brown and dried out.

Q. How are Gattinaras different from Barolos and Barbarescos?
A. Gattinaras come from the northern Piedmont and are made from the same grape, Nebbiolo (locally called the Spanna) and tend to be richer and less astringent. Gattinaras represent excellent value. Top producers are Mario Antoniolo, Brugo, Luigi Nervi, Travaglini and Antonio Vallana.

Q. Does the Piedmont produce a light, easy to quaff dry red wine?
A. Yes. Dolcetto is made in a light, easy to drink style that draws comparisons to Beaujolais. It is cherry red in color, light in body, fruity and must be drunk young. Dolcetto d'Alba is the most popular.

Q. What is the Piedmont's most extensively planted red grape?
A. Barbera with Barbera d'Asti (DOC) and Barbera del Monferrato the two most popular. Barberas are made in a variety of styles from light to verging on the robust. Many of the best Barolo and Barbaresco producers make Barberas.

Q. What are two other quality Piedmont dry red wines?
A. Grignolino (Grin-yo-lean-no) (from the grape of the same name) and not often found on restaurant wine lists or, in wine shops. It is grown in several Piedmont regions, but the most popular comes from vineyards in the Monferrato hills near Asti called Grignolino d'Asti. Ghemme (Ghem-may) made from the Nebbiolo grape (locally called Spanna) is easily confused in taste and style with Gattinara.

BARDOLINO
(Bar-doe-*leen*-o)

VALPOLICELLA
(Vol-pole-ee-*chel*-la)

REGION OR DISTRICT:
Veneto, northern Italy, northwest of Verona.

PRINCIPAL GRAPE:
Corvina (Cor-*veen*-ah) and other grapes.

COLOR:
Light ruby red inclining to garnet with age.

BOUQUET:
Fruity with the suggestion of tart strawberries; hints of spice.

TASTE:
Dry, light-bodied, fresh and fruity with almost a suggestion of sweetness.

BEST CLUES:
Tart strawberries on the nose.

SERVE WITH:
White meats, grilled fish, light pastas, hamburgers.

WHEN TO DRINK:
Great years: 1–3 years (94, 90).
Good years: 1–2 years (93, 92, 91).

SERVE AT:
55°–60°F.

NOTES: Although Valpolicella and Bardolino are made from about the same combination of grapes, Valpolicellas usually have more color, body and fruit. Both Valpolicella and Bardolino are delightful, fruity, easy to drink wines that are Italy's answer to Beaujolais. Look for these wines with the bottle designation "Classico" or "Classico Superiore" which means the wine should be of a better quality than just plain Valpolicella or Bardolino.

Valpolicella is also made in a bigger style: Amarone (dry) and Recioto (sweet). These wines need some bottle age and are more expensive.

Some well-known producers of Valpolicella and Bardolino are: Bertani, Bolla, Paolo Boscaini, Masi, Guerrieri-Rizzardi, Luigi Righetti, Sartori, Tedeschi, and Zonin.

GATTINARA

BARDOLINO
VALPOLICELLA

•Milan   Verona•

Turin
•

BAROLO
BARBARESCO

LAMBRUSCO

•Bologna

•Florence
CHIANTI

BRUNELLO DI
MONTALCINO
VINO NOBILE DI
MONTEPULCIANO

MONTEPULCIANO
D'ABRUZZO

•Rome

•Naples

Italian
Red Wines

BRUNELLO DI MONTALCINO

REGION OR DISTRICT:
Southern Tuscany around the
town of Montalcino.

PRINCIPAL GRAPE:
Brunello, a strain of the
Sangiovese grape.

COLOR:
Cherry to ruby red; develops
orange rim with age.

BOUQUET:
Hints of pepper; earthy; spicy;
raisins.

TASTE:
Medium body with earthy quali-
ties and a slightly bitter aftertaste.

BEST CLUES:
Hints of pepper, raisins; acidic
bite on the aftertaste.

WHEN TO DRINK:
Great years: 1–10 years from date
of vintage (94, 90, 88, 85).
Good years: 1–5 years from date
of vintage (93, 91, 89).
Poor years: (92, 84).

SERVE WITH:
Beef, game, lamb and spicy
pastas.

SERVE AT:
60°–68°F.

NOTES: Brunello is one of Italy's most expensive red wines. It is made
from the Brunello grape, a strain of Sangiovese grape (see Chianti) and
is aged in oak for a minimum of 3½ years.

Wine writers are wildly split on its quality, some claiming it divine
and others charging mediocrity and over-pricing. With respect to its
quality, my experience falls somewhere in between. Like every style of
wine, Brunello has its mediocre versions, but the better wines can be
quite good when not drunk too old which is too often the case. Rou-
tinely they do not climb the heights of great Bordeaux, Burgundies,
and California Cabernets, but the best can reach those levels.

Some of the better-known producers are: Altesino, Poggio Antico,
Argiano, Castello Banfi, Biondi Santi, Canalicchio di Sopra, Capanna-
Cencione, Caparzo, Casanova dei Neri, Castelgiocondo, Col d'Orcia,
Costanti, Il Greppone Mazzi, Il Poggione-Franceschi, Lisini, Mastrojan-
ni, Nardi, Talenti, and Val di Suga. There are many other fine producers.

Q. Why are so many Brunellos disappointing?

A. Like Barolos and Barbarescos, they are often drunk too old. These wines (like most wines) cannot handle and do not improve with the excessive bottle age that too many vintners and wine writers recommend. Most Brunellos are at their best within 5 to 7 years of their vintage. Remember, by the time they are bottled they are already a minimum of 3½ to 4 years old. If you then decide they need more bottle age, give it to them, but at least try them sooner rather than later and decide what best suits your palate.

Q. What is Rosso di Montalcino?

A. It is a wine made from grapes from the Brunello vineyards that either doesn't quite measure up to Brunello or from a mediocre vintage. Rosso di Montalcino has DOC appellation.

CHIANTI CLASSICO RISERVA
(Key-*ahn*-tee *Class*-ee-co Ree-*sairv*-ah)

REGION OR DISTRICT:
Northern Tuscany, central Italy.

COLOR:
Ruby red; turns garnet and
browns with age.

TASTE:
Tart and fruity with light tannin
when young; light to medium
body; dry and fruity with age;
slightly harsh or bitter taste and
aftertaste.

WHEN TO DRINK:
Great years: 2–6 years from vin-
tage date (94, 90, 88, 85).
Good years: 1–3 years from vin-
tage date (93, 92, 91).
Poor years: (89, 87, 86).

PRINCIPAL GRAPE:
Sangiovese (Sahn-jo-*vay*-zay).

BOUQUET:
Earthy and smokey; tobacco;
herby; spicy; raisins.

BEST CLUES:
Earthy with slightly bitter aftertaste.

SERVE WITH:
Italian spicy dishes of meat or
cheese, veal, chicken, pastas with
red sauces.

SERVE AT:
60°–65°F.

NOTES: Chianti is a blend of several grapes with Sangiovese repre-
senting 70% or more of the blend. There are over 200 classified vineyards producing Chianti Classico, so the range in tastes and styles is
virtually limitless. Chianti is associated with straw-covered bottles, but
the best is shipped in Bordeaux-shaped bottles designated "Chianti
Classico Riserva." They have an ability to improve with some bottle age
but most should be drunk within six years of the vintage.

P. Antinori, Brolio, Fossi, Melini, Nozzole, and Ruffino are some of the
bigger and better known procers, but there are many other excellent
Chiantis including Badia a Coltibuono, Capannelle, Castello D'Albola,
Castello di Gabbiano, Castello di Uzzano, Castello di Volpaia, Fonterut-
oli, Fontodi, Frescobaldi (Rufina), Gavignano Nippozzano, Giunti, Mon-
santo, Ricasoli, Saccardi, San Felice, Villa Cafaggio and Villa Cerna.

Q. The word "Classico" following the word Chianti means what?
A. It signifies an area of special historical importance within the overall Chianti region that lies between Florence and Siena. Chianti Classico is usually of a higher quality than a wine simply labeled Chianti.

Q. What other fine red wines come from the hills surrounding Florence?
A. Twenty-five or so miles west of Florence is the DOC of Carmignano whose wines have been admired for centuries. From the hills east of Florence comes Chianti Rufina. The Frescobaldi family produces a first-class Chianti Rufina Reserva called Castello di Nipozzano and both red and white Pomino.

Q. What does DOC on a bottle of Italian wine indicate?
A. It is a guarantee of origin, not of quality.

Q. What does DOCG mean?
A. It is a guarantee of origin and controls in the wine making and should be a cut above in quality.

Q. What is the derivation and meaning of the ancient proverb: "A Good Wine Needs No Bush?"
A. In ancient times when very few could read or write, a sign outside a tavern with a bush or a garland of ivy on it meant to the traveler that good wine was served there. Just why the bush evolved as the symbol of good wine is not entirely clear, but it probably derived from the wreath of ivy with which Bacchus was crowned, and which is often shown twined around his staff. Over time the expression "A Good Wine Needs No Bush" came to be synonymous with a good product needs no advertising.

LAMBRUSCO
(Lahm-*brus*-ko)

REGION OR DISTRICT:
Emilia-Romagna, north central Italy just below Piedmont and Veneto.

COLOR:
Various shades from pink to cherry red.

TASTE:
Sweet and semi-sweet; sparkling or fizzy with a slightly bitter after-taste.

WHEN TO DRINK:
Immediately upon purchase. Lambrusco wines imported into the United States do not improve with age.

PRINCIPAL GRAPE:
Lambrusco (Lahm-*brus*-ko).

BOUQUET:
Soda pop.

SERVE WITH:
Alone or with fish or white meats.

SERVE AT:
45°–58°F.

NOTES: In its native habitat of Emilia, Lambrusco is often dry or just slightly sweet with a fizz or effervescence that comes from its natural fermentation. There is a dry, non-effervescent, style that is found in Italy, but the style of Lambrusco imported to the United States is sweet and, to the wine connoisseur, it is nothing more than a sweet "pop" wine. If you like your wine sweet with a fizz or sparkle, you are going to want to try Lambrusco. After all, the "best" wine is the wine you like best.

Some better known importers of Lambrusco are: Cella, Chiarli, Giacobazzi, Leonardini, Riunite.

Q. Is Lambrusco produced only in the Emilia-Romagna region?
A. No. This grape grows throughout Italy, but the best comes from Emilia-Romagna.

MONTEPULCIANO D'ABRUZZO
(Mawn-tay-pul-*cheon*-no Da *bruzz*-oh)

REGION OR DISTRICT:
Abruzzi—along the Adriatic coast.

COLOR:
Medium to dark red.

TASTE:
Rich; chocolatey; blackberry
fruit with hints of spice on the
aftertaste.

WHEN TO DRINK:
Great years: 3–10 years (90, 88,
87, 86, 85).
Good years: 2–6 years (94, 93, 91).
Poor years: (92).

PRINCIPAL GRAPE:
Montepulciano (Mawn-tay-pul-
cheon-no).

BOUQUET:
Spicy; peppery; blackberries.

BEST CLUES:
Pepper and blackberries on the
nose.

SERVE WITH:
Pastas with marinara sauces,
sausage, grilled meats and game.

SERVE AT:
62°–68°F.

NOTES: Montepulciano D'Abruzzo is one of Italy's best kept secrets. It usually sells for under $10 a bottle retail and the overall quality is high. At its best it has a peppery, brambly bouquet with a full, rich spicy taste reminiscent of a first-class Zinfandel. If you are not familiar with Montepulciano D'Abruzzo, try it. It is a reasonably priced wine that deserves to be better known.

Barone Cornacchia, Illuminati, Leonardini, Elio Monti, Emidio Pepe, Casal Thaulero, Cantina Sociale di Tollo, Mezzanotte, Tonino Cataldi Madonna, Valentini, and Ciccio Zaccagnani are some of the better known producers.

Q. Is Montepulciano D'Abruzzo the same as Vino Nobile Di Montepulciano?
A. No! They are entirely different, made from different grapes, in different regions of Italy, and have nothing more in common than that they are Italian red wines.

VINO NOBILE DI MONTEPULCIANO
(*Vee*-no No-*bile* dee Mawn-tay-pul-*cheon*-no)

REGION OR DISTRICT:
Southern Tuscany at the town of Montepulciano about 45 miles south of Siena, central Italy.

COLOR:
Ruby red.

TASTE:
Dry; medium body; tart with slightly bitter aftertaste.

WHEN TO DRINK:
Great years: 2–6 years from date of vintage (90, 88).
Good years: 1–3 years from date of vintage (94, 93, 92, 91).
Poor years: (89).

PRINCIPAL GRAPE:
Prugnolo Gentile, a strain of the Sangiovese grape.

BOUQUET:
Mushrooms; earthy; spicy.

BEST CLUES:
Earthy with slightly bitter after-taste.

SERVE WITH:
Pastas, roast or grilled chicken, red meats, cheeses.

SERVE AT:
60°–65°F.

NOTES: The ancient town of Montepulciano sits on top of a volcanic rock hill surrounded in season by verdant vineyards. DOC law requires that its wines be barrel-aged for at least 2 years. Well made wines from this appellation are similar in style to fine Chiantis. It should not be confused with Montepulciano D'Abruzzo, a red wine from vineyards along the Adriatic coast.

Here is a list of quality producers: Avignonesi, Villa Banfi, Bindella, Boscarelli, La Braccesca Cecchi, Frederico Carletti's Poliziano, Dei, Fassati, Fattoria del Cerro, Fattoria Fognano-Talosa, Gracciano, Ruffino, Tenuta Trerose and Vechia Cantina di Montepulciano.

Q. What is Rosso di Montepulciano?
A. It is a new (1989) appellation that allows producers to sell under this appellation the wines that don't measure up to Vino Nobile.

PESQUERA
(Pess-*care*-ah)

REGION OR DISTRICT:
Ribera del Duero. About 35 miles east of Valladolid in west-central Spain.

COLOR:
Brilliant cherry-red.

TASTE:
Light tannins, smooth and almost always ready to drink. An intense long lasting array of fruit flavors on the palate and aftertaste.

WHEN TO DRINK:
Great years: 4–12 years (94, 91, 89, 86, 85).
Good years: 2–6 years (93, 92, 90, 88, 87).
Poor years: (84).

PRINCIPAL GRAPE:
Tempranillo (Tem-pra-*knee*-oh), known locally as the Tinto Fino.

BOUQUET:
A blend of spices, pepper and vanilla; musty, earthy.

BEST CLUES:
Pepper and vanilla bouquet.

SERVE WITH:
Game, beef, lamb, roast or grilled fowl.

SERVE AT:
62°–68°F.

NOTES: Pesquera is one of the world's great wines. It has an intensity of taste and bouquet that rival the best Bordeaux. It is produced along with its neighbor, Vega Sicilia, in what was until recently geographical isolation. Pesquera's original vineyards (new vineyards have been extensively planted) are on a plateau with a stunning view of the plains of Spain. The vines grow in soil covered with smooth, round stones that in ancient times formed the bed of the Duero River (called the Douro in Portugal) that now flows about a half mile to the east of the vineyards.

Pesquera's proprietor, Alejandro Fernández, founded his winery just a little over 20 years ago.

Pesquera is made from 100% Tempranillo grapes, known locally as the Tinto Fino. The wine is fermented in stainless steel tanks and then aged for about 2 years in American oak. For several years Pesquera experimented with French oak but found that the Tempranillo grape was better suited to American oak. Year after year Pesquera delivers a high quality wine.

Q. What are some other quality wine producers of the Ribera del Duero region?
A. Ismael Arroyo, De Mollina, Penalba Lopez, Valduero, Perez Pascvas, Urbion Crianza, Vina Mayor, Mauro, Vina Pedrosa, Vega Sicilia and wines made by a local cooperative that sell under the label of Penafiel.

Q. Is each vintage the same in this region of Spain?
A. No.

RIOJA RESERVA
(Ree-*o*-ha Ray-*zerv*-ah)

REGION OR DISTRICT:
Rioja, Northeastern Spain.

COLOR:
Light to medium red.

TASTE:
Dry; slightly roasted flavor; light
to medium body; old Riojas can
have a woody-oaky aftertaste.

WHEN TO DRINK:
Great years: 3–7 years (94).
Good years: 1–5 years from date
of vintage (93, 92, 91, 90, 89).

PRINCIPAL GRAPE:
Tempranillo (Tem-pra-*knee*-oh).

BOUQUET:
Musty or earthy; vanilla;
mushrooms; slightly cedar-like.

SERVE WITH:
Lamb, beef, roast chicken, stews.

SERVE AT:
62°–68°F.

NOTES: The Rioja district is located along a 75 mile stretch in Northeastern Spain and makes some of Spain's finest red wines. Reservas must be aged at least one year in oak and not less than two in the bottle. Gran Reservas spend two years in oak and a minimum of three years in the bottle. Although a variety of Rioja styles are made, it is the reservas and gran reservas that should have your attention. Riojas get so much barrel and bottle age, they are usually ready to drink when purchased. The youngest Riojas are labeled either crianza or sin crianza meaning with or without oak. Riojas are still relatively inexpensive and usually represent good value.

Some of the larger and more prestigious Rioja producers of are Berberana, Bilbainas, CVNE, Marqués de Cáceres, Conde De Salceda, Campo Viejo, Contino, Domecq, Franco-Espanolas, Faustino, Montecillo, Muga, Marqués de Murrieta, Olarra, Federico Paternina, Privilegio, Marqués de Riscal, La Rioja Alta and Santiago. Some lesser known but fine Riojas are Martinez Bujanda, Muerza, Remélluri, and Tondonia.

TORRES GRAN CORONAS
(MAS LA PLANA)
"BLACK LABEL" RESERVA

REGION OR DISTRICT:
Penedès in Catalonia is located about a 40 minute car drive south of Barcelona.

COLOR:
Dark red.

TASTE:
Fruity with rich hints of spice with a long and pleasing after-taste.

WHEN TO DRINK:
Great years: 5–20 years (94 93, 91, 90, 89, 88, 87, 85).
Good years: 3–10 years (83, 82, 81).
Poor years: (92, 86, 84, 80).

PRINCIPAL GRAPE:
Cabernet Sauvignon (Cab-air-*nay* So-veen-*yawn*) 100%.

BOUQUET:
Black cherries, fruity, earthy.

BEST CLUES:
Spicy fruit.

SERVE WITH:
Red meats, game, roast fowl, pastas in red sauces.

SERVE AT:
62°–68°F.

NOTES: Torres Gran Coronas (Mas La Plana) "Black Label" Reserva is one of the world's great wines and has earned that distinction in blind competition. The 1970 Black Label, in what was dubbed the "Wine Olympics," was declared the winner over several classified Bordeaux mega-weights. Other Torres red wines include Sangre de Toro (Bull's Blood) and Coronas and in the Reserva line: Gran Sangre de Toro, Gran Coronas, and Vina Las Torres. The whites are labeled Vina Sol, Gran Vina Sol, Vina Esmarlaldo and Vina Las Torres. In the single vineyard category: Fransola "Green Label" and Milmanda. Other quality Catalonian wines exported to the United States are Jean Leon, René Barbier and Raimat.

VEGA SICILIA UNICO RESERVA
(Veg-ah Si-sil-yah Un-*ee*-ko Ray-*zerv*-ah)

REGION OR DISTRICT:
Ribera Del Duero, about 30 miles east of Valladolid in west-central Spain.

COLOR:
Deep red with touches of brown on the rim.

TASTE:
Hints of spice or pepper on the palate with a lingering aftertaste.

WHEN TO DRINK:
Great years: On release (91, 89, 86, 85, 83, 82, 81, 76, 73).
Good years: On release (93, 92, 90, 88, 87, 80, 79, 78, 76, 75, 74).
Poor years: (84, 77).

PRINCIPAL GRAPE:
Tempranillo (Tem-pra-*knee*-oh).

BOUQUET:
Fruity; hints of cedar and tobacco; a touch of oxidation; high acidity.

BEST CLUES:
A slight tobacco nose and an intense taste.

SERVE WITH:
Red meats, game, fowl.

SERVE AT:
62°–68°F.

NOTES: Vega Sicilia is the most expensive wine of Spain and has a history that pre-dates its neighbor Pesquera, having been founded in 1864. The usual varietal blend for Vega Sicilia Unico Reserva consists of about 60% Tempranillo (known locally as Tinto Fino), 25% Cabernet Sauvignon, Malbec and Merlot and 5% of a white grape known as the Albillo. Unico is a full-bodied wine with a high alcohol content (13.5%) and receives an incredible 10 years or more of age in American and French oak and in the bottle before being offered for sale.

Q. Is Unico Reserva the only wine made by Vega Sicilia?
A. No. Until 1986 a younger style Vega Sicilia called Valbuena was made. Since 1991 the winery has produced a wine called Alion made from 100% Tempranillo grapes.

CABERNET SAUVIGNON
(Cab-air-*nay* So-veen-*yawn*)

REGION OR DISTRICT:
California.

COLOR:
Medium to dark red; most well made Cabernets are a dark ruby when young; brown rim indicates significant age.

TASTE:
Berry-like; mint; bell pepper; dry; tannic when young; soft and smooth with maturity; medium to full-bodied; herbaceous finish.

WHEN TO DRINK:
Great years: 4–15 years (94, 92, 91, 90, 87, 86, 85, 84).
Good years: 2–7 years (93, 89).
Poor years: (88).

PRINCIPAL GRAPE:
Cabernet Sauvignon (Cab-air-*nay* So-veen-*yawn*).

BOUQUET:
Minty; herby; blackcurrants; eucalyptus; cassis; chocolate; oaky-spicy.

BEST CLUES:
Eucalyptus or blackcurrants bouquet.

SERVE WITH:
Roast beef, steaks, osso buco, lamb, game, roast fowl such as pheasant, duck, goose, steaks, cheese.

SERVE AT:
62°–68°F.

NOTES: Recent competitive tastings of well-made California Cabernet Sauvignons have proven that the best can hold their own with the best from France. Many of the most promising California Cabernet Sauvignons are being made by wineries less than 20 years old. Cabernet Sauvignon improves with bottle age, but, unfortunately, because most can be drunk with pleasure within three to five years of their vintage, they have not developed the "aging track record" of their French counterparts. For those who can wait until they reach their best, the rewards are great. Mature Cabernets are hard to find and expensive when available.

Here is a list of California wineries by county or region known for quality Cabernet Sauvignons, but there are wineries not listed that make fine Cabernets, and part of the fun is in discovering them:

El Dorado: Boeger.

Lake County: Guenoc.

Livermore Valley: Concannon, Wente Bros.

Mendocino: Fetzer and Husch.

Modesto: E&J Gallo.

Monterey: Durney, Morgan, Monterey Vineyards, Smith & Hook.

Napa: S. Anderson, Beaulieu, Beringer, Buehler, Burgess, Cain, Cakebread, Caymus, Chappellet, Chateau Potelle, Chimney Rock, Clos du Val, Clos Pegase, Clos Robert, Conn Valley, Consentino, Cuvaison, Dalla Valle, Diamond Creek, Dominus, Duckhorn, Dunn, Far Niente, Forman, Franciscan, Freemark Abbey, Girard, Grace Family, Grgich Hills, Groth, Hawk Crest, Heitz, Hess Collection, La Jota, Judd's Hill, Mayacamas, Merryvale (Profile), Robert Mondavi, Chateau Montelena, Monticello Cellars, Mount Veeder, Newton, Opus One, Pahlmeyer Proprietary, Robert Pepi, Joseph Phelps, Plam, Raymond, Rombauer, Rutherford Hill, Saintsbury, V. Sattui, Seltzner, Sequoia Grove, Silver Oak, Silverado, St. Clement, St. Supéry, Shafer, Spottswoode, Stag's Leap Wine Cellars, Sterling, Sutter Home, Swanson, Philip Togni, Truchard, Trefethen, Viader, Vichon, La Vieille Montagne, and ZD Winery.

Paso Robles: Eberle, J. Lohr, Peachy Canyon, Wild Horse.

Santa Barbara: Firestone, Foxen, Gainey.

Santa Cruz: Cinnabar, Ridge, Mount Eden, Santa Cruz Mountain.

Sonoma: Alexander Valley Vineyards, Arrowood, Belvedere, Benziger, Buena Vista, Carmenet, Chalk Hill, Chateau De Baun, Chateau Souverain, Clos du Bois, B.R. Cohn, Domaine Michel, Dehlinger, DeLoach, Dry Creek, Estancia, Gary Farrell, Ferrari-Carano, Fisher, Foppiano, Geyser Peak, Gundlach-Bundschu, Hanna, Hanzel, Haywood, Iron Horse, Jordan, Kendall-Jackson, Kenwood, Kunde Estate, Lambert Bridge, Laurel Glen, Matanzas Creek, Mazzocco, Murphy-Goode, Preston, Ravenswood, Seghesio, Simi, Smothers Brothers, Chateau Souverain, St. Francis, Chateau St. Jean, M.G. Vallejo, and Viansa.

Yuba: Renaissance Vineyard and Winery.

Q. Do quality Cabernet Sauvignons of fine vintages improve with age?

A. Yes, and continue to develop for years. Big age-worthy California Cabernet Sauvignons can handle extensive bottle age as well or better than Grands Crus Bordeaux.

GAMAY BEAUJOLAIS
(Gam-ay *Bo*-sjo-lay)

GAMAY NOIR
(Gam-ay *Nwahr*)

NAPA GAMAY

REGION OR DISTRICT:
California. Grows best in cool counties such as Napa, Sonoma and Monterey.

COLOR:
Light to medium red.

TASTE:
Light-bodied, fruity with low tannins.

WHEN TO DRINK:
Within 1 to 3 years of the vintage (94, 93, 92, 91).

PRINCIPAL GRAPE:
Gamay Beaujolais (a clone of Pinot Noir); Napa Gamay or Gamay Noir (a clone of the Gamay grape).

BOUQUET:
Light, refreshing fruit scents —raspberries, strawberries, cranberries.

BEST CLUES:
Fruit scents.

SERVE WITH:
Hamburger, chicken, veal, steak, grilled fish and seafood.

SERVE AT:
55°–62°F.

NOTES: Gamay Beaujolais should not be confused with the other California varietal known as Napa Gamay or Gamay Noir, which is made from the same grape that makes Beaujolais. It is terribly confusing! Gamay Beaujolais is a clone of the Pinot Noir grape but rarely develops the richness of flavor of the Pinot Noir.

Most Gamay Beaujolais and Gamay Noirs are made in a fresh, light, fruity style with low tannins. They are to be enjoyed young and should be served chilled.

Some of the better known Gamay Beaujolais producers are:

Mendocino: Dunnewood, Fetzer, and Parducci.

Monterey: Emerald Bay and Monterey Vineyards.

Napa: Beaulieu, Beringer, Inglenook, and Robert Pecota.

Paso Robles: Castoro Cellars, Jan Kris.

Sonoma: Geyser Peak, Glen Ellen, Pedroncelli, Sebastiani, Buena Vista, and Weinstock.

Well known Gamay Noir or Napa Gamay producers are:

Napa: Charles Shaw and Wermuth.

Sonoma: Buena Vista, Coturri, Geyser Peak, and Preston.

Q. What does "estate bottled" on a California wine label mean?
A. It must contain only wine bottled at the vineyard where the grapes were grown.

Q. What does the designation "California" on a wine label mean?
A. 100% of the grapes were grown and fermented in California.

Q. Where did Robert Louis Stevenson spend his honeymoon in 1880?
A. Napa Valley. First in the Springs Hotel in Calistoga, and then in a bunk house in an abandoned Silverado mine on Mount St. Helena. Stevenson called the wines "bottled poetry . . . The smack of California earth shall linger on the palate of your grandson."

MERLOT
(Mair-low)

REGION OR DISTRICT:
California.

COLOR:
Medium to medium-dark ruby
with purplish tinges when young.

TASTE:
Rich, ripe fruit flavors; medium
tannin; fruity lingering aftertaste
with a hint of vanilla.

WHEN TO DRINK:
Great years: 3–8 years (94, 93,
91, 90, 87, 86, 85, 84).
Good years: 2–5 years (89).

PRINCIPAL GRAPE:
Merlot (Mair-low).

BOUQUET:
Plummy; spicy; minty; tea.

BEST CLUES:
Plummy, spicy bouquet with rich
soft fruit tastes.

SERVE WITH:
Beef dishes, lamb, pheasant,
quail, duck, grilled sausages,
grilled scallops.

SERVE AT:
60°–68°F.

NOTES: Until about ten years ago Merlot was used in California primarily as a blending grape. It is now the "hot" red varietal. California Merlots have less tannins and are softer than Cabernet Sauvignons but have not yet achieved the complex nuances of bouquet and taste that the best Cabernets exhibit.

Here are some Merlots that merit your attention:

Alameda: Rosenblum.

Lake: Guenoc.

Monterey: Monterey Vineyards, Smith & Hook.

Napa: Beringer, St. Clement, Clos du Val, Clos Pegase, Cosentino, Cuvaison, Duckhorn, Franciscan, Freemark Abbey, Jaeger Family, Robert Keenan, Liparita, Markham, Matanzas Creek, Merryvale, Robert Mondavi, Monticello, Napa Creek, Newton, Pahlmeyer, Robert Sinskey, Rutherford Hill, St. Clement, Silverado Vineyards, Shafer, Stag's Leap Wine Cellars, Sterling, Swanson, Truchard, and Turnbull.

Paso Robles: Peachy Canyon, Tobin James, and Wild Horse.

Santa Barbara: Gainey, Firestone, Fess Parker, Santa Ynez.

Santa Cruz: Ridge Vineyards.

Sonoma: Alexander Valley, Arrowood, Benziger, B.R. Cohn, Chateau Souverain, Clos du Bois, Dry Creek, Ferrari-Carano, Gary Farrell, Hacienda, Hanna, Murphy Goode, Kendall-Jackson, Kenwood, Kunde, Lambert Bridge, Mill Creek, Rabbit Ridge, Ravenswood, St. Francis, Domaine St. George, and Chateau St. Jean.

Q. What French Rhône and Italian grapes have become popular with California winemakers?

A. The first California vintner to show a major interest in Rhône wines was Randall Grahm who became known as the Rhône Ranger. Now a number of California wineries are growing such Rhône grapes as the Grenache, Cinsault, Mourvedre, Carignane, Marsanne, Roussanne, Viognier, and making good and interesting wines. Tuscany's Sangiovese grape has also become a popular recent planting. Atlas Peak, Benziger "Imagery Series," Estancia, Martin Bros' "Il Polio," Seghesio, Shafer's "Firebreak," Flora Springs, Swanson, Viansa, and Villa Ragazzi are fine examples.

Q. How long should you age fine wine?

A. Until the wine is right for you. The best way to find out when a wine is ready to drink is to drink a bottle from time to time and keep notes. When it's right to your taste, you'll know it. But even then there is no hurry to drink it up. When a fine wine reaches its best, it doesn't suddenly plunge into decline. It will usually stay at this "best" plateau for several years.

PETITE SIRAH
(Puh-*teet* Sir-*ah*)

SYRAH
(Sir-*ah*)

REGION OR DISTRICT:
California.

PRINCIPAL GRAPE:
Petite Sirah (Duriff); Syrah.

COLOR:
Dark red.

BOUQUET:
Raspberries; pepper; plums;
blackberries.

TASTE:
Full-bodied, with lots of mouth-puckering tannins when young.
Rounds out and develops soft,
rich fruit after about five years.

BEST CLUES:
Raspberries on the nose, rich
taste of fruit on the palate and
aftertaste.

WHEN TO DRINK:
Great years: 5–10 years (94, 92,
91, 90, 87, 86, 85, 84).
Good years: 3–7 years (93, 89, 88).

SERVE WITH:
Hearty red meats such as roast
and grilled beef and lamb.

SERVE AT:
62°–68°F.

NOTES: Petite Sirah is *not* made from the famous grape of the Northern Rhône, the Syrah, but from a lesser known Rhône grape called the Duriff that is no longer grown in any French vineyard entitled to Appellation Contrôlée. A recent study at the University of California at Davis suggests, however, that the Petite Sirah is not made exclusively from the Duriff but from a combination of different varietals.

California wines labeled "Syrah" are made from the same grape that produce the famous wines of Côte Rôtie and Hermitage.

California Petite Sirahs and Syrahs are usually big, hearty, robust wines that need bottle age to be drinking at their best. Until recently, neither the Petite Sirah nor the Syrah were popular varietals and often were used as blending wines. The secret to the personality development of these wines is in sufficient bottle age. If drunk too young, they taste tannic and tart, even bitter, and show none of the blackberry, raspberry, plummy scents and flavors that develop with proper bottle age. A good example was Parducci's 1980 Petite Sirah. When tasted in 1984 the tannin dominated the fruit and it was harsh. When last drunk in late 1988 it was a rich, full-bodied wine with explosive scents and tastes of blackberries and plums.

Some well known producers of *Petite Sirah* are:

Alameda: Rosenblum.

El Dorado: Sierra Vista.

Livermore Valley: Chouinard and Concannon.

Lake County: Fortino, Guenoc.

Marin: Thackery.

Mendocino: Parducci.

Napa: La Jota, Stag's Leap Wine Cellars, Stags Leap Winery and Turley Cellars.

Santa Barbara: Qupé.

Santa Cruz: Hecker Pass, Mirassou and Ridge.

Sonoma: Christopher Creek, Dry Creek, Field Stone, Foppiano, Hop Kiln, Topolos at Russian River, and Windsor.

Yolo: Bogle.

Producers of *Syrah* are:

Alameda: Rosenblum, Edmunds St. John.

Amador: Karly, Sobon Estate.

El Dorado: Sierra Vista.

Marin: Thackery.

Mendocino: MacDowell, Prager Estate, Parducci.

Napa: Jade Mountain, Joseph Phelps, Swanson and Truchard.

Paso Robles: Eberle, Meridian, Wild Horse.

Santa Barbara: Cambria, Fess Parker, Qupé, Sunstone, Zaca Mesa.

Santa Cruz: Bonny Doon and Ridge.

Sonoma: Alderbrook, Benziger "Imagery Series," Christopher Creek, Dry Creek, Duxoup, Geyser Peak, Field Stone, Foppiano, Kendall-Jackson, Preston, Rabbit Ridge and Windsor.

Yolo: R. H. Phillips.

PINOT NOIR
(*Pee*-no *Nwahr*)

REGION OR DISTRICT:
California. (See also Oregon).

COLOR:
Light to medium red.

TASTE:
Light to medium bodied with overtones of cherries with a lingering spice on the finish.

WHEN TO DRINK:
Great years: 3–8 years (94, 93, 92, 91, 90, 87, 86, 85).
Good years: 2–3 years (89, 88).

PRINCIPAL GRAPE:
Pinot Noir (*Pee*-no *Nwahr*) 100%.

BOUQUET:
Berry-like aromas of cherries; vanilla; hints of spice.

BEST CLUES:
Berry-like aromas of cherries.

SERVE WITH:
Grilled meats, veal, roast or grilled chicken, cornish game hen, grilled salmon, swordfish or tuna.

SERVE AT:
60°–65°F.

NOTES: Pinot Noir is the grape that makes the great red Burgundies. Over the years California vintners have struggled with this varietal with varying degrees of success. In the last five or six years there has been a marked improvement in the overall quality and a number of California Pinot Noirs equal and some better their more celebrated Burgundian namesakes.

Some well known producers are:
Marin: Kalin.
Mendocino: Greenwood Ridge, Husch, Navarro.
Monterey: Chalone, Morgan.
Napa: Acacia, Bouchaine, Carneros Creek, Clos du Val, Cosentino, Cuvaison, Étude, Kent Rasmussen, Robert Mondavi, Mont St. John, Newlan, Saintsbury, Robert Sinskey, Truchard and ZD.
Paso Robles: Creston, Tobin James, Wild Horse.
San Luis Obispo (Arroyo Grande and Edna Valley): Edna Valley,

Talley.

San Benito: Calera.

Santa Barbara: Au Bon Climat, Babcock, Byron, Calera, Cambria, Foxen, Gainey, Fess Parker, Sanford, Santa Barbara Winery, and Zaca Mesa.

Santa Cruz: David Bruce, Mount Eden and Santa Cruz Mountain Vineyard.

Sonoma: Alexander Valley Vineyards, Benziger, Clos du Bois, Chateau De Baun, Chateau Soueverain, Davis Bynum, Dehlinger, Davis Bynum, Durney, Ferrari-Carano, Gary Farrell, Greenwod Ridge, Hanzell, Kendall-Jackson, Kenwood, Kistler, Pedroncelli, Pellegrini, Rochioli, Schug, Williams-Selyem, Robert Stemmler, Rodney Strong, and Joseph Swan.

Q. Do all wines improve with age?
A. No. Most wines (more than 90%) should be consumed when bottled and released. Only the pedigree wines of fine vintages improve with age.

Q. What are varietal wines?
A. They are wines named after the grapes from which they are made, e.g., Chardonnay, Zinfandel, Pinot Noir, Cabernet Sauvignon, Sauvignon Blanc.

Q. What is the most important factor that determines a great vintage?
A. The weather. The other wine components remain essentially the same: the grapes, the soil, the winemakers, the vinification methods.

Q. What does "vintage" mean?
A. Vintage is the year the grapes were picked and crushed, so every year, good or bad, is a vintage year. However, not every wine producer vintage dates his wines every year. If the vintage was bad, he may decide to blend it with other wines of other years in which case it is not given a vintage date. Most jug or generic wines are blends of different grapes of several years and do not carry vintage designations.

ZINFANDEL
(Zin-fan-dell)

REGION OR DISTRICT:
California.

PRINCIPAL GRAPE:
Zinfandel, usually 100%.

COLOR:
Light to dark red with purple
tinge when young.

BOUQUET:
Raspberries; spicy-berry;
peppery; earthy; briary; alcoholic.

TASTE:
Berry-like; plummy; light to
full-bodied depending on style;
moderate acidity and tannin;
often tart but fruity.

BEST CLUES:
Spicy-berry bouquet; berry-like
with tart taste and aftertaste.

SERVE WITH:
Hamburgers, steaks, rack of
lamb, chicken, spicy pastas, stews,
venison, barbecues, pizza.

WHEN TO DRINK:
Great years: 3–8 years (94, 92,
91, 90, 87, 85, 84).
Good years: 2–5 years (93, 89).
Poor years: (88).

SERVE AT:
60°–65°F.

NOTES: Until about 15 years ago this uniquely California grape was used primarily for blending. Now it is the second most popular red grape varietal after Cabernet Sauvignon. Zinfandels vary considerably in style, from light to full-bodied and in color from deep purple to pink. Full-bodied Zinfandels can improve considerably with age and when ten or more years old often take on a Bordeaux quality. Most of the better Zinfandels are made in the cool climates of Sonoma, Napa and Mendocino Counties with Amador County Zinfandels attracting wide attention.

Alameda: Rosenblum, Edmunds St. John.

Amador: Amador Foothill, Karly, Montevina, Renwood, Shenandoah Vineyards, Sobon Estate and Story.

El Dorado: Sierra Vista, Lava Cap.

Lake County: Guenoc.

Livermore Valley: Concannon.

Mendocino: Edmeades, Fetzer and Parducci.

Monterey: Morgan.

Napa: Beringer, Buehler, Burgess, Cakebread, Caymus, Clos du Val, Chateau Montelena, Chateau Potelle, Cuvaison, De Moor, Deer Park, Elyse, Franciscan, Grgich Hills, Lamborn Family, Mayacamas, Robert Mondavi, Chateau Montelena, Newlan, Joseph Phelps, V. Sattui, Shafer, Sky Vineyard, Sterling, Storybook Mountain, Sutter Home, Traulsen, and Turley Cellars.

Paso Robles: Creston, Eberle, Peachy Canyon, Tobin James and Wild Horse.

San Luis Obispo (Arroyo Grande Valley): Saucelito Canyon.

Santa Cruz: Ridge.

Sonoma: Benziger, Cline Cellars, Coturri, DeLoach, Dry Creek, Ferrari-Carano, Gary Farrell, Ernest & Julio Gallo, Gundlach Bundschu, Haywood, Hop Kiln, Kendall-Jackson, Kenwood, Kunde, Limerick Lane, Lytton Springs, Mazzocco, Pedroncelli, Preston, Quivira, Rabbit Ridge, Rafanelli, Ravenswood, St. Francis, Sausal, Sebastiani, Seghesio, Simi, Joseph Swan, Chateau Souverain, Topolos, Williams-Selyem, and Windsor.

When you find a Zinfandel producer and style you particularly like, stock in a case or two. The "word" has a way of getting out and spreading on a full-flavored, reasonably priced Zinfandel.

Q. If you were to buy a red Zinfandel off the shelf without knowing anything about it, what might you expect?
A. Red Zinfandels cover the full gamut of styles and tastes, from light to medium to full-bodied, with medium-bodied, rich, spicy wines being the rule. Big, robust, full-bodied, age-worthy Zinfandels are still made but in far less profusion than medium-bodied Zinfandels.

Q. What are some of the better known robust, age-worthy Zinfandels.
A. Lytton Springs, Rafanelli, Ravenswood, Ridge, Rosenblum, Storybook Mountain.

Q. When is the optimum time for drinking red Zinfandels?
A. Most Zinfandels are at their best in their youth and should be drunk within 2 to 6 years of their vintage. Some of the big, age-worthy Zinfandels gain in complexity and nuances beyond this time and can develop for 10–20 years. With substantial bottle age, these big Zinfandels often take on the nuances of an elegant Bordeaux.

WHITE ZINFANDEL/BLUSH

ROSÉ WINES

REGION OR DISTRICT:
California.

COLOR:
Pink; rosé; blush or the "eye of the partridge."

TASTE:
Semi-sweet to sweet.

WHEN TO DRINK:
When released or within 1 to 2 years of the vintage.

PRINCIPAL GRAPE:
Zinfandel (Zin-fan-dell) and other red grapes.

BOUQUET:
Tropical fruit; suggestions of licorice.

BEST CLUES:
Pink or blush color; slightly sweet to sweet.

SERVE WITH:
As an aperitif or with fish, white meats, vegetable casseroles, veal and mild cheeses.

SERVE AT:
45°–52°F.

NOTES: White Zinfandel has proved phenomenally popular in the United States with sales of about a hundred million bottles per year. It is typically made with some residual sugar or sweetness. Because the Zinfandel grape is red, white Zinfandels usually have a slight pinkish tint. The degree or depth of pinkness or "blush" depends on how long the grape skins remain in contact with the crushed juice. Blush wines are also made from red grapes other than the Zinfandel such as Pinot Noir, Cabernet Sauvignon, Gamay, Granache, Merlot, Barbera, etc.

These wines are fresh, fragrant and made for easy drinking. Some well known producers of white Zinfandels and "blush" wines are:
Livermore Valley: Wente.

Amador: Shenandoah.

Lake County: Konocti.

Mendocino: Fetzer.

Monterey: Emerald Bay.

Napa: Beringer, Buehler, Inglenook, Robert Mondavi, and Sutter Home.

Paso Robles: Castoro Cellars, Creston, Harmony Cellars, Jan Kris and Laura's Vineyard.

San Joaquin: Delicato.

Santa Barbara: Santa Barbara Winery and Firestone.

Santa Cruz: Sarah's Lane.

Solano: Lost Hills.

Sonoma: Glen Ellen, Hop Kiln, Kenwood, De Loach, Pedroncelli, Sebastiani, Seghesio, Stone Creek, M.G. Vallejo, and Weinstock.

Q. What winery started the White Zinfandel revolution?

A. Sutter Home went from a production of 15,000 cases in 1981 to about 3 million cases twelve years later.

PINOT NOIR
(*Pee*-no *Nwahr*)

REGION OR DISTRICT:
Willamette Valley and Umpqua Valley, Oregon.

COLOR:
Light red to dark ruby.

TASTE:
Medium tannins; light to full-bodied; suggestion of sweetness with a spicy aftertaste.

WHEN TO DRINK:
Great years: 2–5 years (94, 92, 90).
Good years: 1–3 years (93, 91, 90, 89, 88).

PRINCIPAL GRAPE:
Pinot Noir (*Pee*-no *Nwahr*).

BOUQUET:
Earthy-smokey; cherries, herbs, spicy.

BEST CLUES:
Earthy-smokey bouquet with a suggestion of sweetness on the palate.

SERVE WITH:
Game, steak, lamb, roast fowl such as quail, pheasant and roast chicken.

SERVE AT:
62°–68°F.

NOTES: The Oregon wine industry in little more than 20 years has carved out a world-class reputation for red wines made from the Pinot Noir grape. In a 1979 blind wine-tasting, a "wine shot" heard around the world occurred when an Oregon winery, Eyrie, bested all but one of several famous Burgundy red wines.

Here is a list of some of the outstanding producers of Oregon Pinot Noirs: Adelsheim Vineyard, Amity, Beaux Freres, Bethel Heights, Bridgeview, Broadley, Cameron, Chateau Benoit, Cristom, Domaine Drouhin, Elk Cove, Evesham Wood, Eyrie, King Estate, Knudsen Erath, Kramer, Lange, McKinley, Montinore, Oak Knoll, Panther Creek, Ponzi, Redhawk, Rex Hill, St. Innocent, Sokol Blosser, Tyee, Yamhill Valley and Willamette Valley Vineyards.

Q. What other well known grapes are grown and wines made in Oregon?

A. Oregon's winemakers have taken on a number of world famous *vinifera* grapes with increasing success including Chardonnay, Gewurztraminer, Pinot Gris, Riesling and to a lesser extent Cabernet Sauvignon and Sauvignon Blanc.

Q. If you were required to spend one year all alone on a deserted island and were allowed to take with you four cases of wines in any combination, two videos, two books and two CDs, what would you take?

A. The answer, of course, will differ with each person, but knowing that my wine allotment is slightly less than a bottle per week, I would take along a vaccu-vin so that after a bottle is opened, it can be drunk over three or four days without spoiling.

CABERNET SAUVIGNON
(Cab-air-*nay* So-veen-*yawn*)

REGION OR DISTRICT:
Columbia Valley, Yakima Valley and Walla-Walla Valley.

COLOR:
Ruby with purple tint when young. Develops brown or orange rim with age.

TASTE:
Moderate tannins when young; full-bodied; fruity and smooth, but with a lean, soft, spicy finish.

WHEN TO DRINK:
Great years: 3–10 years (94, 89, 88).
Good years: 2–5 years (93, 92, 91, 90).

PRINCIPAL GRAPE:
Cabernet Sauvignon.

BOUQUET:
Cassis, blackcurrants, plums, vanilla.

BEST CLUES:
Blackcurrants and spices.

SERVE WITH:
Lamb, beef, grilled or roast chicken, game, pastas, sausage.

SERVE AT:
62°–68°F.

NOTES: Although Washington State makes a full range of wines from *vinifera* grapes, Cabernet Sauvignon arguably makes its best wine with Merlot a close second. Well-made Cabernet Sauvignons from the Columbia, Yakima and Walla-Walla Valleys have distinct styles and tastes and are recognized as world-class wines.

Washington's largest viticultural region is the Columbia Valley Appellation that extends from its northern boundary south to Oregon. The two premier wine appellations are the Yakima Valley and Walla-Walla Valley. Yakima Valley, Washington's first approved viticultural area, begins at the foothills of the Cascade Mountains and extends east to the Kiona Hills. The Walla-Walla Valley vineyards are in the southeastern part of the state bordering Oregon. A number of viticulturists believe that Walla-Walla Valley holds the potential for becoming one of the world's great wine-growing areas.

Some of the premier wineries making outstanding Cabernet Sauvignons are: Chateau Ste. Michelle, Columbia Crest, Columbia Winery, L'École No. 41, Hogue Cellars, Kiona Vineyards, Latah Creek, Leonetti Cellar, Quilceda Creek, and Woodward Canyon.

Q. What other popular European varietal wines are made in Washington?
A. Chardonnay, Chenin Blanc, Gewurztraminer, Merlot, Riesling, Sauvignon Blanc, Semillon.

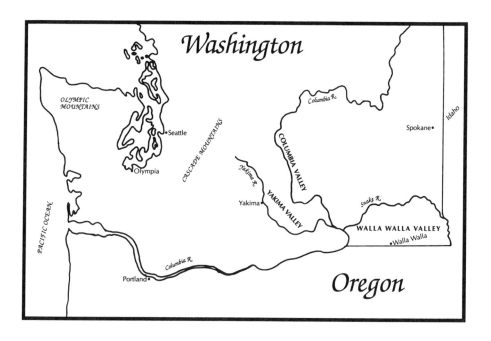

MERLOT
(Mair-low)

REGION OR DISTRICT:
Columbia Valley, Yakima Valley
and Walla-Walla Valley.

COLOR:
Crimson to ruby red.

TASTE:
Soft tannins; medium-body;
smooth with a fruity or spicy
finish or aftertaste.

WHEN TO DRINK:
Great years: 3–6 years (94, 91,
89, 88).
Good years: 1–4 years (93, 92, 90).

PRINCIPAL GRAPE:
Merlot (Mair-low).

BOUQUET:
Cherry scented; herbs;
blackcurrants.

BEST CLUES:
Cherry and blackcurrant scents.

SERVE WITH:
Red meats, grilled chicken,
grilled salmon, and game.

SERVE AT:
62°–68°F.

NOTES: The Merlot grape has adapted well to the viticultural areas of Washington and has become that state's second most popular red wine. As in California, here a soft, rich, easy to drink wine is made but without the intensity of flavors and complex nuances of Cabernet Sauvignon.

Some of the better-known producers of Merlot are Arbor Crest, Blackwood Canyon, Bookwalter, Chateau Ste. Michelle, Chinook, Columbia Crest, Columbia Winery, Hogue Cellars, L'École No. 41, Leonetti Cellar, Miletstone, Andrew Will Cellars, Woodward Canyon.

Q. Washington has three appellations: Columbia Valley, Walla-Walla Valley and Yakima Valley. What percentage of grapes must come from these appellations in order for the appellation name to be used on the label?
A. 75% and, in order to use the state name, 95% of the grapes must come from Washington.

EAST COAST

Since the 17th century wine has been made from grapes grown in vineyards along the east coast of the United States. A few years before the American Revolution, Thomas Jefferson, George Washington and other prominent Virginians of that day were members of a group formed by an Italian immigrant, Philip Mazzei, to make wine from vineyards adjacent to Monticello. Until after World War II, when modern sprays made it possible to control insects and diseases, it proved impossible to grow the *Vitis vinifera*—the classic European grape varieties—successfully.

CONNECTICUT: In Connecticut **Charmard**, which makes only *vinifera* wines, **Haight**, and **Hopkins** vineyards are three of the leading producers.

GEORGIA: The two leading wineries producing *vinifera* wines with a special emphasis on Chardonnay and Cabernet Sauvignon are **Chateau Elan** and **Habersham Vineyards and Winery**.

MARYLAND: **Boordy Vineyards**, **Catoctin Vineyards and Winery** and **Elk Run Vineyards** make a wide range of fine wines, and **Basignani Winery** makes a Chardonnay of outstanding quality.

MASSACHUSETTS: **Westport Rivers Vineyards and Winery** is producing some interesting Chardonnays, Rieslings and Pinot Noirs.

NEW JERSEY: In the Garden State, **Kings Road Vineyard** deserves recognition for its Chardonnay and Pinot Noir and **Unionville Vineyards** for Riesling.

NEW YORK: Following the repeal of Prohibition in 1933, the largest concentration of vineyards was located in upstate New York around the Finger Lakes. Today, with nearly 100 wineries, New York State is second only to California in wine production in the United States.

Initially wine was made from local grapes of the species *Vitis labrusca*, but a strong foxy or grapey taste caused these wines (with the exception of sparkling wines) to be unacceptable to dry wine drinkers. Starting in the mid-1940's, hybrids (crosses between American *Vitis labrusca* and European *Vitis vinifera*) were successfully grown. The first *vinifera* wines were made in New York in the 1960s.

Persistence and improved viticultural techniques increased the acreage of successful *vinifera* vineyards, and today lighter style first-class Chardonnays and Rieslings are coming from such Finger Lakes wineries as **Wagner, Fox Run, Hermann J. Wiemer, Heron Hill, Dr. Frank's Vinifera Wine Cellars, Casa Larga, Swedish Hill** and **Hunt Country Vineyards**. A number of wineries make interesting sparkling wines including Glenora and Chateau Frank.

Some of New York's best red wines come from vineyards located within a two-hour drive from Manhattan. In less than 20 years, 13 vineyards have spread across Long Island's North Fork from Riverhead to Peconic, and three other wineries have found homes on the South Fork, known as the Hamptons. In the more temperate climate of Long Island, such classic *vinifera* grapes as Cabernet Sauvignon, Merlot and Chardonnay not only thrive but excel, and vintners here have high hopes for Cabernet Franc. Most of the wines from this viticultural region are worthy of your attention but look for Cabernet Sauvignons from **Hargrave, Mattituck Hills** and **Pindar**; Chardonnays from **Gristina, Jamesport, Lenz, Palmer** and **Pugliese**; Merlots from **Bedell, Bidwell, Jamesport, Paumanok** and **Pindar**.

NORTH CAROLINA: Two wineries not to be overlooked are **Biltmore Estate Wine Co.** and **Westbend Vineyards**.

NORTHERN NEW ENGLAND: The weather is too cold in Maine, New Hampshire and Vermont for the widespread growing of wine grapes, but wineries in these states make some interesting fruit wines. **Bartlett** in Maine has become well known for its blueberry wines. In Vermont **Joseph Cerniglia** produces over 50,000 gallons of various apple wines.

PENNSYLVANIA: **Allegro** and **Chaddsford** are well known for their production of first class Chardonnays and Cabernet Sauvignons. With nearly 50 wineries, Pennsylvania is worth exploring for a wide variety of wines.

RHODE ISLAND: **Sakonnet** is the leading winery with a range of *vinifera* wines including Chardonnay and Pinot Noir.

VIRGINIA: Thomas Jefferson's statement that wine "should be made here and we have every soil, aspect and climate of the wine countries" is being proved by the more than 40 wineries in his native Virginia. Here *vinifera* grapes are making some outstanding wines. Some of the whites showing best are lovely scented Chardonnays from **Barboursville, Montdomaine, Oasis** and **Prince Michel**, and floral, full flavored Rieslings from **Meredyth** and **Rapidan** River. The **Williamsburg Winery** makes quality Cabernet Sauvignon, Merlot and Chardonnay. **Horton Vineyards** is a new winery that is coming on with varieties such as Viognier, Marsanne and Mourvèdre.

MIDWESTERN STATES

ARKANSAS: **Wiederkehr Wine Cellars** makes a broad range of wines.

ILLINOIS: **Lynfred Winery** for Chardonnay.

INDIANA: **Oliver Wine Company** for Riesling, Merlot and Gewurztraminer.

MICHIGAN: **Fenn Valley** for Riesling; **Chateau Grand Traverse** for Chardonnay, **Mawby Vineyards and Winery** for Pinot Gris and Pinot Noir, and **Tabor Hill Winery** for a variety of wines.

MISSOURI: The standouts are **Blumenhof Vineyards, Stone Hill Wine Co., St. James Winery**, and **Mount Pleasant Winery**.

OHIO: Wineries that have made their marks are **Chalet Debonné** for Chardonnay and Riesling, **Firelands Wine Co.** for Riesling and Champagne, and **Markko Vineyards** for Chardonnay, Riesling and Cabernet Sauvignon.

WISCONSIN: The **Wollersheim Winery** for Chardonnay, Riesling and Pinot Noir.

WESTERN STATES

ARIZONA: The winery setting this state's wine standards is **Sonoita** for Cabernet Sauvignon and Merlot.

HAWAII: The oldest winery in Hawaii is **Tedeschi Vineyards** on the island of Maui. The vineyards grow near the top of a precipice overlooking beautiful Maui Bay and the Pacific Ocean. A first-rate Beaujolais style wine is made from the Carnelian grape. If you are visiting Maui, the view of the ocean and the surrounding country-side from the vineyards is worth a trip to the winery.

IDAHO: **Ste. Chapelle** is famous for its Chardonnay and a leader in Idaho.

NEW MEXICO: At last count New Mexico had 20 bonded wineries producing a full-range of wines from *vinifera* and hybrid grapes. Two of the best known are **Gruet Winery** and **La Chiripada Winery**.

TEXAS: In recent years there has been a renewed interest in *vinifera* grape growing and winemaking, and a number of wineries are making a complete range of top quality wines. These include **Cap Rock Winery** for Sauvignon Blanc; **Fall Creek Vineyards** for Chardonnay, Sauvignon Blanc and Cabernet Sauvignon; **Llano Estacado** for Chardonnay, Johannisberg Riesling, Cabernet Sauvignon, and Merlot; **Messina Hof** for Cabernet Sauvignon, "Angel" Johannisburg Riesling, Gewurztraminer and Chardonnay; and **Pleasant Ridge** for Chardonnay, Cabernet Sauvignon, and Chenin Blanc.

MADEIRA

REGION OR DISTRICT:
Island of Madeira off the west
coast of Africa.

COLOR:
Pale gold to deep amber.

TASTE:
Caramel; butterscotch; raisins,
nutty; rich; dry to sweet depending on grape variety.

WHEN TO DRINK:
When purchased.

PRINCIPAL GRAPE:
Sercial, Verdelho, Bual and
Malmsey.

BOUQUET:
Burnt; raisins; caramel; alcoholic.

BEST CLUES:
Slightly burnt bouquet; nutty;
caramel taste.

SERVE WITH:
Sercial as an aperitif; Malmsey
after dinner.

SERVE AT:
55°–62°F.

NOTES: In making Madeira, the fermentation process is stopped by the addition of brandy. This fortification produces wines of varying sweetness with an 18%–21% alcohol content. Then a curious process is followed. The wine is slowly heated in *estufa* tanks to temperatures of 120°F or more. It is then blended by the *solera* method (see Sherry).

There are four principal types of Madeiras, named after the grapes from which they are made. Sercial (*Sair*-see-al) is the driest. Verdelho (*Vair*-del-o) usually has a slightly higher degree of sweetness. Bual (*Boo*-al) is sweet and Malmsey (*Maums*-ee) is rich and the sweetest. Madeiras are the longest lived of all wines. Though not vintaged today, very old vintage Madeiras are occasionally available at wine auctions such as those held at Christie's and Sotheby's. A recently opened Madeira was proof that the extent of their longevity exceeds a century.

Blandy Brothers & Co., Cossart Gordon & Co., Harveys, Henriques & Henriques, Leacock & Co., and Rutherford & Miles are well known producers.

Q. Madeira is a fortified wine. What has been the source of brandy used to fortify Madeira?
A. Sugar cane which grows abundantly on the island of Madeira.

Q. Is the Estufa system of heating wines unique?
A. Yes. No other wine in the world is subjected to such a heating process.

Q. What is the origin of Malmsey?
A. Malmsey is reputed to come from Crete in the form of the Malvasia (Mal-va-*zee*-ah) grape.

Q. What is the origin of Sercial, the dryest Madeira wine?
A. Sercial is believed to have originated from the German Riesling.

Q. What is the origin of the Verdelho vine?
A. Verdelho is believed to be a cross between the Pedro Ximenes of Spain and the Verdea of Italy.

VINTAGE PORT

COUNTRY:
Portugal, Upper Douro.

COLOR:
Ruby red; loses color with age.

TASTE:
Fruity and sweet; faintly nutty flavor; smooth, rich and mellow; sometimes a peppery finish.

WHEN TO DRINK:
Great years: 10–25 years (94, 92, 91, 85, 83, 77, 70, 66, 63).
Good years: 8–15 years (93, 90, 87, 82, 80, 78, 75).

PRINCIPAL GRAPE:
Varied.

BOUQUET:
Alcoholic; fruity; cherries; plummy; peppery.

SERVE WITH:
After dinner by itself or with apples, walnuts, Stilton or bleu cheeses; as a nightcap.

SERVE AT:
65°–68°F.

NOTES: Port is a fortified wine, having had its fermentation stopped by the addition of grape brandy. Vintage Port is a blend of the best wines of an exceptional year. In contrast to other ports, Vintage Port is matured in barrels for about 2 years and then bottled. It continues to mature in the bottle for a long time depending on the quality of the vintage, but even Vintage Port has age limitations. Because it develops a thick crust (sediment) while acquiring bottle age, the bottle should be stood up a week or more before opening and then carefully decanted. If the crust slips free and mixes with the wine, pour it through a Melitta coffee filter when decanting.

Cockburn, Croft, Delaforce, Dow, Fonseca, Graham, Quinta do Noval, Sandeman, Taylor Fladgate and Warre are the best known shippers of Vintage Port but there are others, such as Martinez, Smith-Woodhouse, Gould Campbell, Calem, Niepoort, C. da Silva and Ferreira.

Q. Are all ports blended?
A. Except for wines from one Quinta (vineyard), all ports are blended. Vintage Port is a blend of the same year but from different vineyards. Ruby, Tawny, and White ports are blends of several years.

Q. Is Vintage Port the only type of port?
A. No. In fact Vintage Port represents a very small portion (about 5%) of the overall port production. Ruby port is a blend of young rich wines and has a deep ruby color. It is the sweetest type of port. Tawny port is matured in casks and represents a blend of different years. Tawny ports normally take on a brown or tawny color after years in the cask. Crusted port is not usually the wine of a single vintage. It is matured in casks and further aged in the bottle and it throws a crust or sediment like vintage port. It needs decanting. White port is made along the lines of Tawny port but made from white grapes and ranges in style from dry to sweet.

Q. What is the Vinho Verde?
A. Vinho Verde (*Veen*-ho *Vair*-day) is the largest wine-producing region in Portugal. It is located in northern Portugal and is responsible for about a quarter of Portugal's wine production. Although almost three-quarters of its production is red wine, Vinho Verde is best known in the United States for its white wines. They should be drunk young.

Q. What does the word "Garrafeira" on a Portuguese wine label mean?
A. It means "reserve" and is supposed to represent the producer's best quality wine bottled only in excellent vintages.

Q. What are some other well known Portuguese wine areas?
A. Setubal, Colares, and Bucelas, all located around Lisbon, and Bairrada and Dao in the north located just south of the Douro mountains where Port is made.

SHERRY, FINO
(Feen-o)

REGION OR DISTRICT:
Jerez (Hair-eth), southern Spain.

PRINCIPAL GRAPE:
Palomino.

COLOR:
Pale yellow to pale amber.

BOUQUET:
Pungent; nutty; suggestion of almonds.

TASTE:
Nutty; almonds or walnuts; slightly smokey; very dry and crisp; biting aftertaste.

BEST CLUES:
Nutty bouquet and taste.

SERVE WITH:
As an aperitif or with foods, especially tapas, canapes or smoked salmon.

WHEN TO DRINK:
When purchased.

SERVE AT:
50°F.

NOTES: Sherry covers a wide spectrum of tastes from bone dry (Fino); Amontillado (Ah-mon-tea-*ya*-do) usually slightly sweet; Oloroso (O-lo-*row*-so) sweet; Cream milk (Brown) very sweet. Sherry is originally fermented out dry, i.e., all of the grape sugar has been converted to alcohol. The wines are then graded. Generally speaking, the best quality wines become Fino Sherries. Sweet Sherries have the sweetness added after the final fermentation. Sherry is fortified with grape brandy which accounts for its high alcohol content—from 15.5% to 20%. Since the *Solera* method of blending is used, it is never a vintage wine. In the *Solera* system, casks are stored in rows on top of one another with the oldest wines in the bottom casks. As wine is removed from the bottom cask, it is refilled from the wine in the cask above it of the same style and type.

Among the more popular dry Sherries are González Byass's Tio Pepe, Pedro Domecq's La Ina, Garvey's San Patricio, Harveys' Bristol Fino, Duff Gordon's Pinta, Emilio Lustau's Jarana, Osborne's Quinta,

LaRiva's Tres Palmas, Sandeman's Cortado and Williams & Humbert's Dry Sack.

Q. How do other types of Sherry differ from Fino?
A. Amontillado has more body and color than Fino and is often produced by cask-aging specially selected Finos. Manzanilla is dry and has a slightly salty taste. Oloroso is full-bodied and dark-golden in color and usually sweet.

Q. How are fortified wines made?
A. The fermentation process is stopped at some point by the addition of brandy. This raises the alcohol level to a point where the yeast cells are anesthetized and fermentation stops, leaving some of the grape sugar which gives sweetness to the wine. Well known examples of fortified wines are Port, Madeira, and Sherry.

Q. How long do fortified wines such as Port, Maderia, and Sherry keep once opened?
A. It depends on the fill of the bottle or the proportion of air to wine. Two-thirds filled should keep several weeks. One-third filled, about a week. Finos should be chilled and drunk the same day when opened.

Q. What is the main source of wine bottle corks?
A. The bark from cork-oak trees with Portugal and Spain are the principal suppliers. The bark is harvested about every 10 years and some trees have been known to yield bark for 250 years.

TOKAY ASZU

COUNTRY:
In northeast Hungary.

COLOR:
Amber.

TASTE:
Honeyed; butterscotch; rich with tangy acidity; bitter aftertaste.

WHEN TO DRINK:
When purchased.

PRINCIPAL GRAPE:
Furmint.

BOUQUET:
Faintly burnt; oxidized with honeyed overtones.

BEST CLUES:
Faintly burnt bouquet; butterscotch taste, acidic bite and bitter aftertaste.

SERVE WITH:
After dinner.

SERVE AT:
55°F.

NOTES: Tokay Aszu is made by a method somewhat similar to French Sauternes and German Trockenbeerenausleses. A portion of the grapes are allowed to become overripe, a condition known as aszu, or better known as *Botrytis cinerea* (noble rot). These raisin-like grapes are then placed in baskets called puttonyos (poo-tawn-yos), crushed and then added to the fermentation of the normal harvest. The neck label on the bottle will show the number (3 to 6) of puttonyos or putts added. The more puttonyos added, the sweeter and more alcoholic the wine.

Q. Is the style of Tokay changing?
A. Yes, but slowly. Tokays made under Communist regimes are known for having a woody and oxidized taste and bitter aftertaste. Unless you like a burnt, cooked, oxidized taste to your wine (and some wine drinkers do) Tokay is a wine to be approached cautiously. Western-European winemakers who have come to Tokay are making a new style that is a fruitier flavored wine.

Q. What was the best vintage in Tokay in the post term years?
A. 1993.

Q. What is Tokay Essencia?
A. Tokay Essencia is the richest and sweetest and contains more residual sugar than a six puttonyos Tokay Aszu. It is aged in cask for 10 years.

Q. Did the ancient Greeks and Romans age their wines in order to improve their quality?
A. Yes. Alexander Henderson in his treatise, *The History of Ancient and Modern Wines* describes their wine cellars: "The casks containing the stronger wines were . . . in general ranged along the walls of the wine cellar and sunk to a greater or less depth in sand. In this situation they were allowed to remain till the wine was judged to have acquired a sufficient maturity."

Q. Were the best ancient wines dry or sweet?
A. Sweet.

WINE DO'S AND DON'TS

DO build your own wine cellar, if possible.

DON'T worry if the temperature doesn't stay at a constant 55°–60°F. Temperatures up to 68°F should present no problems provided they are relatively constant and without severe fluctuations.

DO try the second least expensive wine on the wine list when dining out. It is often the restaurant's best wine value.

DON'T order hard liquor before dinner. Hard liquor dulls the palate.

DO read as many good wine books and wine newsletters as you can.

DON'T become a wine snob.

DO buy the 1990, 1989, 1988, 1986, 1985, and 1982 red Bordeaux if you can afford them.

DON'T buy the 1993, 1992, and 1991 Bordeaux unless there is a specific reason. These are weak vintages.

DO serve your red wines at room temperature, but be sure it is not over 68°F.

DON'T serve white wines too cold. It masks their bouquet and flavor.

DO object if the waiter brings you a wine other than exactly as you ordered.

DON'T always reject the wine if it is not exactly as ordered. It is better to have a comparable wine than none at all.

DO drink red wines with red meats and white wines with white meats, but,

DON'T be afraid to challenge this addage to suit your tastes.

DO pay attention to vintage charts.

DON'T be a slave to vintage charts. Even poor years have their successes, but if you buy a wine of a poor vintage have a reason for doing it.

DO provide pencils and paper at your wine tastings.
DON'T allow smoking.

DO decant and allow the wine to breathe when appropriate.
DON'T worry about what the decanter looks like so long as it is clean
and free of odor.

DO stand a bottle of mature red wine up long enough before decanting
to allow the sediment to settle to the bottom.
DON'T shake or jiggle the bottle when decanting.

DO drink all types of wines; red and white, sweet and dry, cheap and
expensive.
DON'T become a "one" type wine drinker such as the Burgundy or
Bordeaux snob.

DO keep wine tasting notes or at least write down the name of that
"wonderful" wine so you can reorder it.
DON'T throw away interesting wine labels.

DO have blind wine tastings.
DON'T invite people who smoke.

DO require the sommelier or waiter to open the wine at your table.
DON'T *ever* accept a bottle of wine that has been opened before being
presented to you. It may have been opened the night before and
become oxidized.

DO serve dry white wines before the red wines.
DON'T use vinegar on any food (not even on salad) when wine is served. Vinegar kills the taste of wine.

GLOSSARY OF TERMS

ACETIC ACID Vinegar; caused by organisms that convert alcohol into acetic acid.

ACIDITY Especially noticeable in the bouquet and taste of white wines. Too much or too little acidity will cause the wine to be out of balance.

AFTERTASTE The taste that is left in the mouth after swallowing. An excellent clue to the wine's identity and quality and close attention should be paid to it.

AOC *Appellation d'Origine Contrôlée* (Ah-pel-ah-see-awn Dor-ee-Jeen Cawn-trol-lay). French laws created by the *Institut National des Appellations d'Origine* regulate virtually everything concerned with the production of wine in France and is organized into three main quality divisions. The best is *Appellation d'Origine Contrôlée* (AOC) and is the most strictly controlled. Next is *Vin Délimité de Qualité Supérieure* (VDQS). The third division is *Vin de Pay* (Van duh Payee) (country wines) which are much less regulated, particularly as regards grape variety and vineyard yield.

APPLE-LIKE A bouquet characteristic of certain wines made from the Chardonnay grape.

BERRY-LIKE A taste characteristic of certain California red wines—especially Zinfandel.

BODY (Light, medium, full)—The fullness of the wine as it feels in the mouth. High alcohol wines and wines made in hot climates tend to be fuller in body.

BOUQUET The complex of a wine's odors; its smell. A wine's most distinguishing feature.

BURNT Derived from the near pasteurization of Madeira or when a wine has become maderized or oxidized from too much contact with air.

CARAMEL A taste characteristic of Madeira and Tokay.

CEDAR, CEDARWOOD The classic bouquet of a fine, mature Bordeaux wine.

DOC Initials that stand for Denominazione di Origine Controllata and are intended to control grape growing and wine making of a higher quality in Italy.

DOCG Denominazione di Origine Controllata e Garantita, a category established in Italy in 1963 for its highest-quality wines.

DRY Absence of sugar.

EARTHY Suggestive of the smell of wet earth.

FERMENTATION The interaction of yeasts with grape sugar converting the sugar into almost equal parts of ethyl alcohol and carbon dioxide gas that escapes into the air.

FINISH Synonymous with aftertaste.

FLINTY The smell of struck flint.

FLOWERY A bouquet characteristic of many fine German wines, especially Mosels and Rheingaus.

FRUITY A fruit-like impression on both the smell and taste. Not grapey.

HERBS, HERBACIOUS A bouquet characteristic of some California wines, especially Sauvignon Blancs.

LEGS Seen on the sides of the wine glass; comes from glycerol in the wine, a by-product of fermentation.

MATURE The wine has acquired just the proper amount of bottle age to be drinking at or near its best.

MINTY A bouquet characteristic of some California and some Australian Cabernet Sauvignons.

NOSE Bouquet, aroma or smell.

OAKY A smell and taste characteristic of white Burgundies and California Chardonnays.

PERFUMED A floral or scented bouquet characteristic of many white wines.

PEPPERY Slightly suggestive of pepper. Prickles the nose or palate.

RIM The color at the rim or edge of the wine in the glass.

SEDIMENT The deposit that forms in the bottle of a well made red wine consisting of precipitates of the wine's components, e.g., tannins, minerals, etc. Usually develops with 5 or 6 years of bottle age.

SWEET The result of residual sugar in the wine, although a dry wine can have a hint of sweetness on the palate.

TANNIN, TANNIC Derived primarily from the grape skins. It acts as a preservative for red wines. When too high it has a mouth-puckering effect but smooths out with bottle age. Red wines lacking sufficient tannin are usually flat and insipid.

VARIETAL The principal grape variety from which a wine is made. For example, red Burgundies are required by French law to be made from 100% Pinot Noir grapes.

INDEX

RIESLING

ARPAD HARASZTHY & CO.
SAN FRANCISCO, CAL.

SAUTERNE

KOHLER & FROHLING

ESTABLISHED 1854.

SAN FRANCISCO.　　　NEW YORK.

CALIFORNIA
Rodensteiner

BACCHUS
VINEYARDS,
SONOMA.

TRAMINER
GRAPE.

RHINE FARM, SONOMA.

Gundlach Bundschu Wine Company Inc.

FORMERLY
J. GUNDLACH & CO.
FOUNDED 1858.

SONOMA,
SAN FRANCISCO
NEW YORK.